MEATLESS RECIPES

Cover art and line drawings by Jane A. Evans

Meatless
Recipes
by
Mattie Louise

Re-Quest Books   Wheaton, Illinois

THE THEOSOPHICAL PUBLISHING HOUSE
Wheaton, Ill., U.S.A.
Madras, India / London, England

First Re-Quest edition published by the
Theosophical Publishing House, Wheaton,
Illinois 60187, a department of the
Theosophical Society in America

—Library of Congress Cat. Number: 75-4315
—ISBN: 0-8356-0463-2

—Printed in The United States of America

Contents

FOREWORD

People are becoming increasingly aware that it is entirely possible, without meat, to have nutritious and taste-satisfying meals, as well as almost endless variety in diet. This development appears to have come about more or less spontaneously, as perhaps one phase of a tentative approach to more intelligent and humane use of our resources. Whatever the individual reasons for foregoing meat—economy, health, ecology, ethical considerations, or moral convictions—more and more people are turning to a nonmeat diet as a solution to their food problems.

Some questions inevitably arise when such an action is taken, for regardless of our aspirations, our thoughts cannot be separated indefinitely from our physical and emotional welfare. "How can I insure an adequate supply of the necessary proteins and other food elements?" "How can I keep from getting bored with a meatless diet?" We need direction and specific guidance. Mattie Louise Gephardt fulfills these needs in this fascinating compilation of interesting, tasteful, and easy-to-follow recipes representing a culinary expertise developed through a lifetime of interest in nutrition and good cookery.

The book is usefully divided into three sections: Protein-rich Recipes (something different for every day of three months!); Cheese and Casseroles (for those who delight in experimentation); and Cottage Cheese and Eggs (for an exciting variety of ways to use these two versatile foods). Whoever browses through this book will want to test its possibilities for promoting robust health and for enlivening and enriching mealtime enjoyment.

Section I
Casseroles & Cheese

Burger Barbecue in Buns

1 can Vegetarian Burger
1 can tomatoes, drained
4 eggs, beaten
1/4 lb. butter
1 onion, chopped
1 green pepper, chopped
1 tsp. oregano
Salt to taste

Saute the onion and green pepper in butter until onion is golden brown. Add burger and drained tomatoes. Cover and simmer over low heat until mixture is steamed through. While still hot, pour the beaten egg over the mixture and stir through gently until eggs are cooked. Add seasonings. Serve on hot buns.

Oriental Patties

4 eggs beaten
1 cup burger
3/4 cup quick oats
1/2 cup onions, chopped
1/4 cup chopped green pepper
1 tsp. salt
1 tsp. soy sauce

Combine ingredients and mix thoroughly. Form into flat patties and fry in oil over low heat. Brown both sides. To complete meal with the oriental theme, serve rice with butter and soy sauce, salad, a green vegetable and a dessert such as peaches and almond wafers.

Tomato Protein Stew

2 cups vegetarian steaklets
2 tbsp. shortening
6 small whole white onions
6 small carrots, cut in half
2 tbsp. flour
1 can condensed tomato soup or brown gravy
1 can water
3 potatoes, quartered
1/4 tsp. whole thyme

Dust steaklets with flour; brown in shortening in large heavy pan. Add soup and water. Cover; simmer 1 1/2 hours. Add remaining ingredients. Cover; cook 1 hour or until vegetables are tender. Stir now and then. To thicken, uncover; cook until desired consistency.

Serves 4.

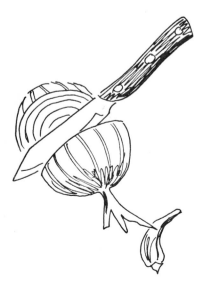

Saucy Steaklet on Rolls

2 tbsp. butter
1/2 cup celery, chopped
1 can condensed tomato soup
1/4 cup water
6 rolls, toasted and buttered
2 cups meat substitute
1/2 cup chopped onion
1-1/2 tsp. chili powder
1 clove garlic, minced
1 tsp. vinegar
1/2 tsp. salt

Melt butter, blend in chili powder and garlic. Add meat substitute; brown lightly; push to one side. Add celery and onion; cook until tender. Stir in soup, water, vinegar, and salt. Cover; cook over low heat for 10 minutes. Uncover, cook an additional 10 minutes. Stir occasionally. Serve on rolls.

Souper Burgers

2 cups burger
1 tsp. shortening
1/4 cup catsup
1 tsp. Worcestershire sauce
6 buns, toasted and buttered
1 cup chopped celery
1 can condensed onion soup
1/2 cup water
1 tsp. prepared mustard
Dash pepper

Saute celery in shortening; stir in burger to separate particles. Add soup, water and seasonings. Simmer 10 to 15 minutes or until slightly thickened. Stir occasionally. Serve on buns.

Serves 6.

Frank-Potato Pie

1 can condensed cream of celery soup
3/4 cup milk
4 cups diced cooked potatoes (about 4 medium)
1/4 cup onion, finely chopped
2 to 3 tsp. prepared mustard
1 cup Vega-links cut lengthwise

Combine soup, milk, onion and mustard. In buttered 11/2 qt. casserole, arrange alternate layers of potatoes, sauce and franks. Cover. Bake in a 400 degrees F oven 30 minutes.

Serves 4.

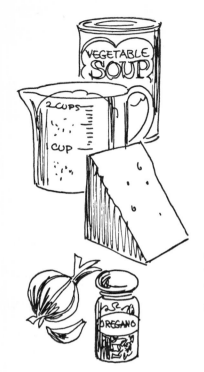

Cheese-Burger Shell Pie

2 cups burger
1 can condensed vegetable soup
1/2 cup shredded sharp Cheddar cheese
1 clove garlic minced
1/8 tsp. leaf oregano

Press burger against bottom and sides of 9 inch pie pan. Mix soup, garlic and oregano; pour into pie shell. Bake in a 350 degrees F oven 15 minutes. Top with cheese; continue baking until cheese melts. When serving, spoon drippings over each portion.

Serves 4.

Golden Mock Chicken Bake

4 cups sliced soymeat (fried chicken style)
2 tbsp. butter
1 tbsp. minced parsley
1 can condensed mushroom soup

Arrange sliced soymeat in single layer in shallow baking dish. Dribble melted butter over it. Stir soup, pour over soymeat; sprinkle parsley on top. Bake 20 minutes 400 degrees F.

Serves 4.

Mock Chicken Croquettes with Sauce

1 can condensed mushroom soup
11/2 cups minced soymeat (fried chicken style)
1/4 cup fine dry bread crumbs
2 tbsp. parsley, minced
1 tbsp. onion, finely minced
1/4 cup milk

Combine 1/3 cup soup with soymeat, 1/4 cup crumbs, parsley and onion. Form into 6 croquettes. Roll in bread crumbs. Chill. Fry croquettes in shortening until thoroughly heated and lightly browned. Blend remaining soup with milk; heat; serve over croquettes.

Serves 3.

Creamed Mock Chicken

1/2 cup celery, chopped
1 can condensed mushroom soup
1/3 to 1/2 cup milk
2 tbsp. butter
1 cup diced soymeat (fried chicken style)
1 cup green peas, cooked
1/8 tsp. ground sage

Cook celery in butter until tender. Blend in other ingredients. Heat; stir often. Serve over split cornbread squares, biscuits or toast.

Serves 3.

5

1-2-3 Mock Chicken Pie

1 cup cubed soymeat (chicken style)
1/2 cup cooked carrots (cut in strips), peas, or cut green beans
1/3 cup of milk
1 tbsp. minced onion
1 cup packaged biscuit mix
1 cup cubed cooked potatoes
1 can condensed mushroom soup
1/4 cup milk
Dash poultry seasoning

Layer soymeat and vegetables in a 1-1/2 qt. casserole. Blend soup, milk, onion, and poultry seasoning; pour over soymeat and vegetables. Bake in a 450 degrees F oven 10 minutes. Meanwhile, combine biscuit mix and milk; roll 1/2 inch thick and cut into 6 or 7 biscuits. Remove casserole from oven; place biscuits on top. Continue baking 15 minutes or until biscuits are browned.

Serves 3 or 4

Creamed Mock Chicken with Almonds over Pancakes

1 cup celery, chopped
2 tbsp. butter
1 can mushroom soup
1/3 to 1/2 cup milk
1 cup diced soymeat, chicken style
2 tbsp. diced pimento
1/4 cup toasted slivered almonds
Pancakes

Cook celery in butter until tender; blend in soup and milk. Add soymeat, pimento and almonds. Heat; stir often. Serve over pancakes.

Serves 4.

Mock Chicken Cacciatore

4 cups soymeat, sliced (chicken style)
1/4 cup seasoned flour
1/4 cup olive oil
8 small white onions
1 medium green pepper, cut in strips
1 can sliced mushrooms, drained
1 small clove garlic, minced
1 can condensed tomato soup
1/2 cup water
2 tbsp. vinegar or lemon juice
1 tbsp. Worcestershire sauce
1/2 tsp. leaf thyme

Dust soymeat slices with seasoned flour. Brown in olive oil; remove from fire. In olive oil and garlic lightly brown onions, green pepper, mushrooms. Blend in remaining ingredients; add soymeat. Cover; simmer about 30 minutes; stir often. Excellent served over spaghetti.
Serves 6.

Peanut Butter Chops

1/2 cup peanut butter
1 cup hot, cooked rice
1/2 cup dry bread crumbs
1/2 tsp. celery salt
1/2 tsp. salt
1 egg, well beaten
3 tbsp. catsup
1/2 tsp. grated onion

Combine all ingredients and form into chops. Place in well greased baking dish and bake 15 or 20 minutes at 375 degrees F, or until brown.
Serves 4.

Curried Mock Chicken with Almonds

2 cups soymeat, sliced
(chicken style)
3 tbsp. seasoned flour
1 can condensed cream
mushroom soup
1/4 cup toasted slivered
almonds
2 tbsp. vegetarian shortening
1/2 tsp. curry powder
1 tbsp. chopped pimento
1/2 or 3/4 cup water

Dust soymeat slices with
seasoned flour, brown in
shortening. Combine
remaining ingredients except
almonds. Pour over soymeat.
Cover, cook over low heat 10
minutes. Stir often; (add a little
more water, if necessary); add
almonds. Cover. Cook 5
minutes more.

Serves 3 or 4.

Chickett Fritters

1 cup diced Chicketts
1/2 cup diced celery
1/2 cup diced onion
1 tsp. Worthington broth
seasoning
3 tsp. baking powder
2 tbsp. butter
3 eggs, well beaten
1 cup milk
1 cup flour
Salt and pepper to taste

Combine Chicketts, celery,
onion, soup base and other
seasonings and braise in butter
for 1 hour over low heat.
Combine milk and beaten eggs,
then add flour, which has been
sifted with baking powder.
Combine Chickett mixture with
milk and egg mixture beating
well. Drop batter by tsp. into
deep fat and fry golden brown.
Serve hot with syrup and
honey.

Chicketts with White Sauce

1 can Chicketts
1 egg, well beaten
1/2 cup milk
2 tbsp. flour
1/2 cup bread crumbs
2 tbsp. fat
Pinch of salt

Mix beaten egg and milk. Add salt. Dip Chicketts in flour, then in egg mixture, then in bread crumbs. Fry in hot fat until nicely browned. Serve with medium white sauce.

Serves 4.

White sauce

3 tbsp. butter
3 tbsp. flour
1 cup milk or other liquid
1/4 tsp. salt

Melt butter, add flour, and blend thoroughly. Add liquid gradually, stirring to avoid lumping. Add salt and heat mixture to boiling point, stirring constantly. This makes thick sauce. More liquid may be added for thinner sauce.

Cheeseburger Loaf

1/2 cup undiluted evaporated milk
3 cups burger
1-1/2 tsp. salt
1 tbsp. catsup
1 egg
1 cup cracker crumbs
2 tbsp. onion, chopped
1 tsp. dry mustard
1 cup American cheese, grated

Blend all ingredients except cheese until thoroughly mixed. Line loaf pan with heavy waxed paper. Place 1/2 cup cheese in bottom of pan; spread mixture evenly. Cover with 1/2 meat loaf mixture. Repeat with remaining cheese and meat layers. Bake in moderate oven 350 degrees F about 30 minutes. Allow loaf to stand about 10 minutes before turning out on platter. Remove paper; slice for serving.

Serves 6.

Vega-Links and Scalloped Potatoes

4 cups potatoes, sliced and cooked
6 Vega-Links, cut in 1 inch pieces
1-1/2 tsp. salt
1/2 cup cubed cream cheese
3 cups milk, thickened with flour to make thin white sauce

Mix cream cheese, potatoes, and Vega-Links. Pour the milk over potatoes and bake until brown, about 10 minutes at 375 degrees F.

Serves 6.

Vegetarian Roast with Yorkshire Pudding

2 cups bread crumbs
1 cup peanut butter
1 small finely chopped onion
2 eggs, well beaten
1 tsp. salt
1 cup mashed potatoes (left over potatoes may be used)
1/2 tsp. savory

Mix all ingredients together and form into loaf. Bake in moderate oven, 350 degrees F for 40 to 60 minutes or until firm. This may be eaten hot or cold. Serve with Yorkshire pudding or tomato sauce.

Yorkshire Pudding

1 cup flour
1/4 tsp. salt
1 cup rich milk
3 eggs, well beaten

Mix flour and salt. Add milk and eggs. Beat vigorously with rotary beater or electric mixer. Cover bottom of baking pan with shortening and heat. When shortening is hot pour 1/2 inch layer of batter over it and bake for 30 minutes in hot oven 425 degrees F, or until pudding is brown, basting occasionally with some of hot fat that rises around sides of pudding. Cut into squares and serve very hot with substitute meat dishes.

11

Tasty Burger and Corn Bread

2 cups burger
3/4 cup chopped onion
1/4 cup chopped green pepper
2/3 cup undiluted evaporated milk
1 pkg. (8 oz) corn muffin mix
2 tbsp. butter
1/2 tsp. chopped garlic
3 tbsp. flour
2/3 cup water
1-1/2 tsp. salt
1/4 tsp. pepper
1 cup cooked green peas.

Mix burger and butter. Set aside. Add onion, garlic and green pepper; cook until onion is clear. Stir in flour; add evaporated milk and water mixed. Cook until thickened, stirring constantly. Add burger, salt and pepper, mix well. Place in 9 inch square pan. Prepare corn muffin batter according to package directions. Pour batter in 1 inch strip around edge of pan. Fill center with peas. Bake in hot oven 400 degrees F for 25 minutes.

Serves 6.

French Loaf

1 loaf (brown and serve) French loaf
1/4 cup chopped stuffed olives
1 can Vega-link
1/2 tsp. horseradish
1/2 tsp. poppy seeds

Cut loaf in 1 inch slices crosswise almost to bottom crust. Spread butter on cut surfaces. Combine remaining ingredients and spread on slices. Place loaf on aluminum foil or baking sheet and bake in moderate oven 375 degrees F for 20 to 30 minutes.

Serve hot.

Vegelona Cups

6 slices Vegelona
1/2 cup sharp Cheddar
cheese, grated
1/2 tsp. onion, grated
2 drops Tabasco
2 cups hot cooked rice
1/2 cup condensed cream of
celery soup
1/3 cup water
Pimento stuffed olive slices

Mix together in a bowl the rice, cheese, soup, water, onion, and Tabasco. Arrange bologna slices in a shallow baking dish (edges of meat may touch, but should not overlap). Put about 1/3 cup of rice mixture in the center of each bologna slice. Top each with olive slices. Set temperature control of oven at broil. Broil about 4 inches from source of heat 5 minutes or until bologna slices curl around filling.

Serves 6.

Fritos Mexican Mock Chicken

2-1/2 cups Fritos corn chips
1 clove garlic, minced
1 cup American cheese,
grated
1 can condensed tomato
soup, diluted
1/2 cup water
1 medium onion, chopped
1 cup soymeat, chicken style
1 tsp. chili powder

Place 2 cups of Fritos corn chips in a 2 qt. casserole. Arrange layers of chopped onion, garlic, soymeat and half of grated cheese over the Fritos corn chips. Pour heated soup with chili powder over ingredients in casserole. Top with remaining Fritos corn chips and cheese. Bake at 350 degrees F for 15 or 20 minutes.

Serves 6-8

Choplet-Pecan Vegetable Loaf

2 tbsp. butter
1 cup ground choplets
1/4 cup green pepper, chopped
1 onion, chopped
1/2 cup celery, finely chopped
2 tbsp. flour
1-1/2 cups milk
1 tsp. salt
2 cups cooked rice
2 cups chopped pecans
2 eggs, beaten
1 cup fine bread crumbs

Saute choplets, green pepper, onion and celery until tender. Blend in flour. Mix all ingredients and place in greased loaf pan. Bake 1 hour at 350 degrees F. Serve with mushroom gravy.

Serves 6.

Mushroom Gravy

1 can mushroom soup
1 tsp. Tastex dissolved in 1 cup hot water
1/2 cup milk

Mix mushroom soup and milk. Add Tastex. Heat and serve.

14

Flying Saucers

6 baked individual pie shells
1/4 cup sugar
1 medium onion, minced
1 tbsp. Worcestershire sauce
7 medium carrots
1/4 cup butter
3 tbsp. butter
1-1/2 cups water
1 tsp. Tastex
6 choplets, halved

Wash and scrape carrots. Cut in 2 inch lengths and cook until tender. Drain. Simmer cooked carrots in syrup made with 1/4 cup butter and sugar until glazed and soft. In a saucepan brown onion. Add butter and let melt. Blend in flour. Slowly stir in water. Cook over low heat until mixture comes to a boil, stirring constantly. Add Worcestershire sauce, Tastex, and halved choplets. Add carrots and syrup. Pour a serving into each of the pie shells.

Serves 6.

Sputnik Stew

1 onion
2 carrots
2 stalks celery
1 tsp. salt
3 or 4 medium potatoes
1 pkg. frozen peas
1 can mushrooms
1 can vegetarian protein (any kind)
1 can mushroom soup

Cook 5 minutes in boiling, salted water, onion, carrots, and celery. Add potatoes (shoe stringed), green peas and cook until tender. Saute in vegetable oil mushrooms and protein meat. Add mushroom soup and simmer for a few minutes.

Serves 6.

15

Chinese Green Pea Chow

2 cups Choplets, diced
2 medium sized onions, chopped
2-1/2 cups bamboo shoots
2 tbsp. safflower oil or corn oil
1 cup mushrooms
1 cup celery, chopped
1 cup water chestnuts
2 cups green peas, rinsed with boiling water
1 tbsp. soy sauce
Salt and pepper to taste

Saute onions in safflower oil until golden brown. Mix diced meat and other ingredients together. Add to the browned onions and simmer under cover for 15 minutes. Remove cover, and cook for 10 minutes over medium fire. Add soy sauce. Stir occasionally.

Serves 6.

Broiled Choplets with Pineapple

8 Choplets (20 ozs.)
4 slices pineapple
2 tbsp. cornstarch
1/4 cup brown sugar
1/2 cup broth from Choplets
1/2 cup pineapple juice
1/4 cup seedless raisins
1 tbsp. butter
1/4 tsp. salt

Blend cornstarch, brown sugar, and salt in a saucepan. Slowly stir in pineapple juice and Choplet broth. Cook over low heat until smooth and thick, stirring constantly. Add raisins and butter. Keep on low heat about 10 minutes. Place Choplets and pineapple on a greased cookie sheet. Brush with melted butter. Brown lightly on both sides under broiler. To serve, put one slice of pineapple between 2 Choplets. Pour sauce on top.

Serves 4.

16

Mock Sea-food Chowder

1/2, 14 oz. can MC, chopped
1/2 tsp. garlic powder
1 medium onion, sliced thin
Dilled onion rings
1 tbsp. flour
2 tbsp. cooking oil
2 cans condensed tomato rice soup
2 cups water
1 small green pepper, chopped
1/2 tsp. salt

Saute chopped MC with onion and green pepper in cooking oil until onion and pepper are tender. Smooth flour into tomato rice soup and add to MC mixture. Add water gradually, and stir in garlic powder. Heat together until slightly thickened. Float dilled onion rings on the chowder. Serve hot in soup tureen.

Serves 6.

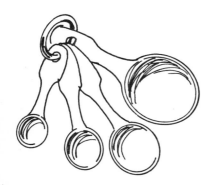

Lentil Patties

2 cups lentil puree
3 tbsp. onions, chopped
1/2 cup walnuts, chopped
2 tbsp. oil
1 tsp. salt

Brown the onion in oil, then mix all the ingredients, and form into patties. Place on an oiled pan, and brown in the oven. Serve with gravy or tomato sauce.

Serves 4.

Millet-Lentil Headcheese

3/4 cup very dry lentil puree
1/4 cup cream
2 eggs
3/4 tsp. sage
1/4 tsp. summer savory
1/3 cup cooked millet
1/2 tsp. salt

Mix all ingredients except eggs, and let stand for 1 hour. Beat egg yolks and whites separately; then carefully fold each into mixture. Put into an oiled bread tin and bake until set. When cold, slice and serve with gravy, or it may be served warm.

Serves 4.

Bean Puree

Cook the beans till the water in which they have been cooking is largely evaporated and the beans are rather dry; then rub them through a puree sieve. (This puree may be served with gravy or tomato sauce, or it may be pressed into an oiled bread tin and baked. Then it can be turned out like a loaf and sliced and served with gravy, tomato sauce, chili sauce or mint sauce.)

Millet Loaf

4 heaping tbsp. hulled millet seed
1 cup water
1 tsp. vegetarian broth
2 tbsp. cooking oil or butter
2 cups carrots, shredded
2 eggs, beaten
2 tbsp. grated cheese
1 tbsp. honey
1 small can green peas
1 tbsp. onion, chopped
Pinch of sweet basil and thyme
Sprig of fresh dill, chopped or 1/8 tsp. crushed dill seeds
1 tbsp. tomato paste
Salt to taste

Soak millet seed in cup of cold water for several hours, drain, and steam with the juice from the peas and the broth until seeds are done. Add the mashed peas, carrots, beaten eggs, tomato paste, onion, fat and seasonings. Blend well, form into a loaf, place in a greased loaf pan, and allow to bake in a slow oven 300 degrees F to 325 degrees for 45 to 60 minutes. About 10 minutes before removing from the oven sprinkle the top of the loaf with the grated cheese and allow to melt. Serve with a green salad or fruit dessert.
Serves 8-10.

The Millet Plant

Millet-Seed Nut Loaf

1/3 cup hulled sunflower seeds, finely chopped
1/3 cup sesame seed meal
1/3 cup walnuts or almonds or pecans, finely chopped
3 eggs, lightly beaten
1-/2 tbsp. melted butter or cooking oil
1-1/2 cups vegetarian broth
Dash of paprika
1-1/2 cups cooked green peas, mashed
1-1/2 cups cooked carrots, chopped
2 tbsp. minced onion or chives
1-1/2 cups soft cooked millet
Salt to taste
2 tsp. lemon juice
1-1/2 cups American cheese, grated

Add the broth and lightly beaten eggs to the millet and combine all ingredients. Pack into a well greased loaf pan, Parmesan cheese on top. Bake in a moderate oven 350 degrees F for 45 minutes, or until firm. Serve with tomato or cream of mushroom sauce.
Serves 8.

Millet-Cheese Nut Loaf

1 cup walnuts, chopped
4 tbsp. sunflower seed meal and sesame seed meal
2 eggs, well beaten
1/3 cup milk
4 tsp. butter or cooking oil
1-1/2 cups American cheese, grated
1 cup cooked millet
2 tbsp. chopped chives or 1 tsp. minced onion
2 tbsp. lemon juice
Dash mace or nutmeg
Salt to taste

Brown onions lightly in fat, add milk, blend into millet. Stir in well beaten eggs, add grated cheese, nuts, seed meals, lemon juice, chives and seasonings. Bake in moderate oven 350 degrees F until cheese is melted.
Serves 6-8.

Millet-Tamale Loaf

1 cup millet meal
3/4 cup Cheddar cheese, grated
4 tbsp. cooking oil
1 clove garlic
4 tbsp. Italian cheese (Parmesan or Romano), grated
1 small can mushrooms
2-1/3 cups canned tomatoes
1 tbsp. onion, minced
3 cups hot water
1/2 cup cold water
Pinch of sweet basil and sweet marjoram
1 tsp. salt

Saute onions in heated oil, add mushrooms and saute lightly, then stir in tomatoes, half of the salt and garlic. Allow to simmer very slowly for about 1-1/2 hours, stirring frequently to prevent sticking. (The garlic clove may be removed after the first 30 minutes, if only a milk flavor is desired.) Then prepare the mush by mixing meal with the cold water, and adding gradually to the salted boiling water, stirring until the mush thickens and bubbles to a boil. Lower the flame and cook over a slow fire for about 12 minutes longer. Place a layer of the mush in the bottom of a greased shallow casserole or baking dish, cover with a layer of the tomato-mushroom sauce, add a third layer of the grated Cheddar cheese, and repeat, ending up with a topping of the mush sprinkled with the grated Italian cheese, making sure to save some of the sauce to serve over the tamale loaf. Bake uncovered in a slow oven 300 degrees to 325 degrees F for about 30 minutes. Serve with a tossed green salad and for dessert an orange custard.

Serves 6-8.

Nut Meat a la King

1tbsp. butter
1/2 cup mushrooms, broken into pieces
1/4 green pepper, chopped
1/4 tsp. salt
1 cup cream
1-1/2 cups diced nut meats
2 tbsp. cream
1 raw egg yolk
1 tbsp. flour or tapioca
1/2 tsp. onion, grated
1/2 tsp. lemon juice
1/4 tsp. paprika

Melt butter, add mushrooms and green pepper, cook. Stir in flour and salt, stirring till it becomes frothy; then stir in cream and continue to stir till it begins to boil. Set in double boiler and add nut meats. Let stand till hot. Beat together egg yolk, cream, onion, lemon juice and paprika. Stir into hot mixture. Serve on toast.

Serves 4.

Bean Loaf

1 cup kidney or yellow-eyed beans
1 tsp. salt
1 tsp. sage
2 tsp. peanut butter
1 tbsp. grated onion
1/4 cup gluten flour
1 tbsp. tomato juice
1 hard-boiled egg, chopped fine

Make puree of the beans, and mix with it the remaining ingredients, stirring the peanut butter smooth with water. Put into an oiled bread pan, and bake till set and browned. Serve with gravy or tomato sauce.

Serves 4.

Vegetarian Nut Loaf

4 cups carrots, grated very fine
1 large onion, finely chopped
1 tbsp. parsley, finely chopped
3 tbsp. melted butter
1 tsp. sage
1 tsp. thyme
1/2 cup fresh green lima beans
5 egg yolks
1/2 cup broken cashew nuts
1/2 cup finely flaked almonds
1-1/2 tsp. vegetable salt

Saute chopped onion in little butter or oil. Beat egg yolks. Combine ingredients. Put in greased baking dish. Bake in moderate oven 45 minutes.

Nut Meat Pie

1-1/2 cups potatoes, diced
1 small onion, chopped
1 tbsp. oil
1 tbsp. flour or tapioca
1 tbsp. parsley, chopped
1-1/2 cups diced nut meat
1 tsp. salt

Boil potatoes in little more than enough water to cover them. Cook onion in oil and add to the potatoes. When potatoes are tender, stir the flour smooth with a little cold water, and stir it into the hot mixture. Add nut meat and parsley, and if mixture seems too thick add hot water. Put into a pan and keep hot. Serve one biscuit on top of each pie.

Serves 4.

Soya Vegetable Stew

1 small bunch celery, chopped
6 cups boiling, salted water
1/2 can green peas
Parsley sprays
1 medium onion, diced
1 rutabaga
1/2 cup Soya Granules
1 turnip, diced
1 tbsp. soy sauce
4 carrots, diced

Cook celery in salted water about 10 minutes. Add carrots, rutabaga, turnip and one large celery core diced, parsley sprays and onion, and soya granules. Cook until vegetables are done; then add 1/2 can peas with 1 tbsp. soy sauce.

Serves 6.

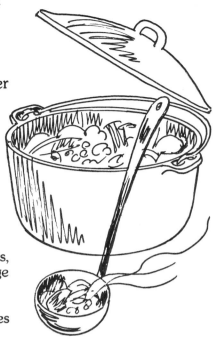

Columbia Loaf

4 hard cooked eggs, chopped
1 qt. bread crumbs
1/2 cup chopped almonds
Tomato juice to make consistency of thick mush
1 tsp. thyme
2 tsp. onion, grated
1 raw egg, beaten
1/4 cup cream
2 tsp. celery salt
1 tsp. salt

Mix thoroughly. Put into an oiled bread pan and bake till set. Serve with cream sauce.

Serves 4.

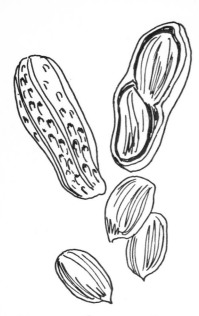

Broiled Peanut Butter-Cheese Sandwiches

1/2 cup creamy peanut butter
1-1/2 cups American cheese, grated
1/2 cup mayonnaise
2 tsp. Worcestershire sauce
1/4 tsp. salt
9 slices white bread
2 medium tomatoes, sliced thin

Combine peanut butter, cheese, mayonnaise, Worcestershire sauce and salt. Toast one side of bread under broiler. Spread untoasted side of bread with peanut butter-cheese mixture. Arrange tomato slices on top. Broil sandwiches until tomato is hot and cheese is melted. Serve immediately. Makes 8 generous servings.

Soya Granules Croquettes

3/4 cup tomatoes, cooked or canned
2 cups Soya Granules Toast crumbs
2 tbsp. soya powder
2 tbsp. onions, minced
1 cup diced celery, cooked

Put minced onions into tomatoes; cook to boil, then add soya powder and cook until thick. Allow to cool. Add Soya Granules and celery. Mix thoroughly and form into croquettes. Dip into toast crumbs and bake on greased tin in moderate oven about 20 minutes. Serve with gravy or sauce.

Serves 4.

Soya Granules Loaf

1 can burger
1/2 cup Soya Granules
1/4 cup bread crumbs
4 tbsp. onion, chopped
1/2 cup milk
2 tsp. salt
1 tbsp. green pepper, chopped
1 beaten egg
1/2 tsp. pepper
1 cup tomatoes, canned
1/2 tsp. celery salt

Mix all ingredients well, kneading with hands. Shape into loaf and bake in greased loaf pan in moderate oven 350 degrees F, until well done or about 1-1/4 hours.

Serves 6.

Soya Granules Casserole

2 cups Soya Granules, cooked
1 cup celery, cooked
1 cup carrots, cooked
2 tsp. powdered vegetable broth
2 tbsp. minced parsley
1 cup stewed tomatoes

Mix ingredients and pour into greased casserole, top with toast crumbs and bake until brown. Dot with butter and serve.

The Soybean

Soya Granules Bean Sprout Patties

2 cups bean sprouts, canned or fresh
1 tbsp. meatlike seasoning
2 to 4 tbsp. milk or tomato juice
1 cup Soya Granules, cooked
2 eggs
1 tbsp. soy sauce
Salt and season to taste

Mix all ingredients and form into patties. Fry or bake until done.

Cashew Timbales

4 green onions, chopped
1 can mushrooms, finely cut
1 cup burger
2 cups cooked natural rice
3 level tbsp. soy flour
1 tsp. Accent
1/2 cup chopped celery
1 cup cashew nuts, coarsely chopped
1/2 can mushroom soup
2 tbsp. oil
Salt to taste
Rusket crumbs

Saute green onions, celery and mushrooms in oil. Add other ingredients; mix thoroughly and allow to cool sufficiently to handle. Form into cone-shaped croquettes and roll in Rusket crumbs. Bake in quick oven to brown and heat through. Serve with favorite gravy.

Serves 6.

Choplets in Swiss Gravy

3 tbsp. shortening
2 medium onions, chopped
1/2 can Choplets
3 tsp. flour
1-1/2 cups water
2 tsp. soy sauce

Simmer chopped onions in shortening. Add Choplets cut into small pieces and simmer until brown. Stir in flour and add warm water, Choplet broth, soy sauce. Allow mixture to simmer until gravy is desired consistency. Serve over mashed potatoes or boiled rice.
Serves 4.

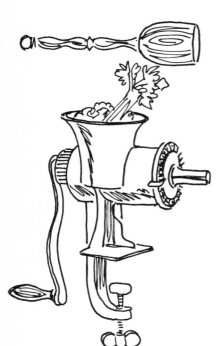

Wham Loaf

3 lb. (2 1-1/2 lb. frozen) sliced Wham
2 13 oz. cans diced Soyameat (chicken style)
1-1/2 green peppers
5 stalks celery
2 medium size onions
8 whole eggs, beaten
2-1/2 cups cornflake crumbs
1 bottle chili sauce
4 tsp. prepared mustard
1 cup light cream
1/2 cup salad oil
1/4 cup Worcester Sauce

Grind together the first five ingredients. Add the rest. Mix all together thoroughly. Bake at 300 degrees F. for 1-1/2 hours.
Serves 12.

Seed Nut Loaf

1/3 cup sunflower seeds, finely chopped
1/3 cup sesame seed meal
1/3 cup almonds or walnuts, finely chopped
1/2 cup lima beans mashed
1/2 cup cooked carrots, chopped
Tbsp. minced onion or chives
4 eggs slightly beaten
1/2 tbsp. butter
1/2 cup milk
1/2 cup whole grain crumbs
1/2 tsp. salt
Tbsp. lemon juice
Dash paprika

Add the milk and lightly beaten eggs to the crumbs and combine all ingredients. Pack into a well greased loaf pan. Bake in moderate oven at 350 degrees F for an hour or until firm. Serve with tomato cream or mushroom sauce.

Serves 4.

Mock Sausage Dish

1 can saucettes
3 peppers, sliced lengthwise
1 medium size onion
1 cup sliced mushrooms
3 medium sized potatoes, quartered
2 cups stewed tomatoes
1 tsp. salt
1/2 tsp. pepper
1 tbsp. oregano

Combine all ingredients in casserole with some of the saucettes on top. Bake at 350 degrees F for 1 hour.

Serves 6.

Choplets Moderne

1 can Worthington Choplets (20 ozs.)
3/4 cup breading meal
1/4 cup grated Parmesan cheese
1 cup tomato sauce (8 oz. can)
1 egg, beaten
Oil for frying
8-10 slices Mozzarella cheese

Preheat oven to 350 degrees F. Grease a large shallow baking pan. Dip choplets in beaten egg and then in breading meal mixed with the Parmesan cheese, coating both sides. Fry in hot oil until browned on both sides. Place in greased baking dish and pour tomato sauce over. Arrange Mozzarella cheese over each serving and sprinkle with additional Parmesan cheese. Bake 15 to 20 minutes.

Serves 8-10.

Mock Salmon Loaf

1 cup Miracle Whip Salad Dressing
2 cups undiluted condensed cream of celery soup
4 eggs, beaten
3 cups chopped onion
1/2 cup chopped green pepper
2 tbsp. lemon juice
2 cans skallops, ground
2 cups fine dry bread crumbs

Combine the salad dressing, soup, eggs, onion, green pepper, lemon juice and mix well. Add skallops and bread crumbs; toss lightly. Place in a well greased loaf pan and bake in moderate oven of 350 degrees F for 1 hour.

Serves 6.

Section II
Cottage Cheese & Eggs

Cottage Cheese Omelet

4 eggs, well beaten
4 heaping tbsp. cottage cheese
1 tbsp. skim milk powder
Dash of salt
Sprinkle of paprika
Pinch of sweet basil

Beat cottage cheese until creamy, stir in milk powder, blending until perfectly smooth. Season and add the very well beaten eggs. (For a fluffier omelet, beat egg yolks and whites separately, folding in the stiffly beaten whites at the very last.) Pour into a buttered omelet pan or heavy skillet and cook over very low heat until browned. If an omelet pan is not used, the omelet must either be turned like a pancake or allowed to finish cooking in a moderate oven, 350 degrees F, after the bottom is lightly browned.

Cottage Cheese Nut Loaf

2 cups cottage cheese
2 cups soft bread crumbs
2 cups chopped nut meats
1-1/2 tsp. salt
1/8 tsp. pepper
1/2 tsp. onion juice
Juice 1 lemon
2 tbs. butter or margarine

Combine all ingredients. Place in well greased baking pan and bake in moderately hot oven (375 degrees F) about 30 minutes. Serve with tomato sauce.

Orange Toast Blintzes

12 thin slices white bread
1/3 cup milk
1 egg slightly beaten
3/4 cup small curd cream style cottage cheese
1 tbsp. sugar
1 tbsp. grated orange peel
1/8 tsp. salt
3 tbsp. melted butter or margarine
2 tbsp. sugar
1 tsp. ground cinnamon

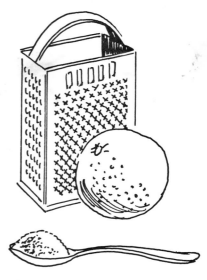

Grease a baking sheet. Trim crust from bread. Brush tops and sides of bread slices with milk. Mix together the egg, cottage cheese, 1 tbsp. sugar, orange peel and salt. Spread about two tbsp. of the mixture evenly over each of six bread slices. Place edges together. Brush tops with melted butter and sprinkle with a mixture of sugar and cinnamon. Place "blintzes" on the prepared baking sheet. Toast in a 400 degree F oven 10 minutes. Serve hot. Garnish with orange slices.
Serves 6.

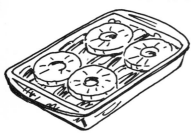

Cottage Cheese and Beef Style Soymeat

1/2 cup milk
1-1/2 cups soft bread crumbs
1 cup cottage cheese
1 egg
1 can sliced beef style soymeat

Combine milk, bread crumbs, cottage cheese and egg, blend well. Mix with soymeat. Put into 10x6x2 inch casserole. Arrange 4 slices pineapple on top and sprinkle with 2 tsp. brown sugar. Bake in 375 degrees F oven until top is lightly browned, 45 to 50 minutes. Serve with raw or pan fried apple rings. Garnish with parsley.
Serves 4.

Lasagne Roll

10 oz. lasagne noodles
1 cup cream style cottage cheese
1 large package (8 oz.) cream cheese
1 large garlic clove, minced
1/2 tsp. salt
1/4 tsp. pepper
2 tbsp. grated Parmesan cheese, divided
2 10-1/2 oz. cans condensed tomato soup
1/2 cup water
1/2 tsp. oregano

Cook lasagne noodles according to package directions; drain. Arrange noodles overlapping 1/2 inch in rectangle container. Meanwhile combine cottage cheese, cream cheese, 1/2 of the minced garlic, salt, 1/8 tsp. pepper, 1 tbsp. Parmesan cheese. Spread mixture on noodles: roll as for jelly roll. Place roll in shallow baking dish (10x6x2) inches. Combine soup, water, oregano, remaining garlic and pepper. Pour over noodles. Sprinkle with remaining Parmesan cheese. Bake in moderate oven 350 degrees F 30 minutes. If desired, serve with additional Parmesan cheese.

Serves 4.

Cottage Cheese Buns

1 cup cottage cheese
1/4 cup finely chopped green pepper
3 tbsp. chili sauce
6 long finger buns

Mix first three ingredients until blended. Split 6 long finger buns almost through. Hollow out part of center, spread with butter. Fill with chili-cheese mixture. Serve cold.

Serves 6.

33

Cottage Cheese Vegetable Casserole

3 cups cooked rice
1 cup milk
1 10 oz. can condensed cream of mushroom soup
2 tbsp. instant onion flakes
1/4 cup sliced stuffed olives
1 cup cottage cheese
1/2 cup dairy sour cream
1 lb. 3 oz. asparagus spears
1/2 cup dried bread crumbs
2 tbsp. melted butter or margarine
1 whole stuffed olive

Combine rice, milk, soup, onion, sliced olives, cottage cheese, sour cream. Reserve six asparagus spears for garnish; cut remainder into 1 inch pieces; stir into rice mixture; turn into buttered 2 qt. casserole. Combine bread crumbs and melted butter; spoon in ring around edge of casserole; arrange reserved asparagus spears spoke fashion on top of rice; place whole olive in center. Bake in moderate oven 350 degrees F 35 to 40 minutes, or until mixture is heated through and crumbs are golden brown.

Serves 6.

French Toasted Cottage Cheese

Make 4 sandwiches (white, whole wheat or rye bread) using 1 cup cottage cheese for filling; then dip each quickly in the French toast mixture below:

2 eggs
1/4 cup milk
Dash of salt.

Beat together with fork in shallow dish. Brown sandwiches on both sides in hot buttered skillet.

Serves 4.

Cottage Cheese Lasagna

2 tbsp. butter
*1/2 19 oz. can vegetarian breakfast links
*20 oz. can vegetarian burger
1 envelope spaghetti sauce mix
1 can tomato paste
1-1/2 cup water
2 tbsp. grated Parmesan cheese
1/2 lb. lasagna noodles
1 lb. cottage cheese
2 tbsp. chopped parsley
1 package (8 oz.) sliced Mozzarrella or Muenster Cheese.

Melt butter in skillet. Cut links into small pieces; cook in skillet over medium heat until brown. Add burger; cook until done, drain fat. Stir in spaghetti sauce mix, tomato sauce, tomato paste, water and Parmesan cheese; simmer 10 minutes. Cook noodles according to package directions; drain; spoon enough sauce into 7x11x2 inches baking dish to cover bottom; lay half the noodles on top; top with half the cottage cheese and half the parsley; cover with sauce. Repeat layers. Cut Mozzarrella or Muenster cheese into wide strips; arrange in cross-bar design on top. Bake in moderate oven 350 degrees F 30 minutes or until cheese melts and sauce is bubbly.

Serves 8.

* Worthington Vegetarian Vega-Links
* Worthington Vegetarian Choplet Burger

Cottage Cheese Noodle Casserole

6 oz. package noodles
1 cup cottage cheese
1 cup sour cream
1/4 cup chopped onion
2 tsp. Worchestershire sauce
1/4 tsp. salt
1/8 tsp. pepper
1/2 cup milk
1/2 cup wheat germ
1/2 cup sharp cheese grated
1 tbsp. wheat germ

Cook noodles according to directions; drain. Mix together cottage cheese, sour cream, onion, Worchestershire sauce, salt and pepper. Stir in milk, then 1/2 cup wheat germ. In greased 1-1/2 qt. casserole arrange cheese mixture and noodles in alternate layers. Sprinkle top with grated cheese and tbsp. of wheat germ. Bake in moderate oven 350 degrees F for 45 minutes.

Serves 4.

Cottage Cheese Quick Patties

1 cup cottage cheese
2 tbsp. shredded Parmesan cheese
1 small can tomatoes
1 package refrigerated crescent rolls.

Blend tomatoes and cottage cheese to prepare a sauce. Separate 1 package crescent rolls into triangles. On four of the triangles evenly spread about 2-1/2 tbsp. tomato-cottage cheese sauce. (see page 38). Top with remaining triangles and press edges with a fork to seal. Place on baking sheet. Sprinkle top of each triangle lightly with shredded Parmesan cheese. Bake at 375 degrees F about 15 minutes or until golden brown. Serve immediately.

Cottage Cheese and Vegetable Casserole-2

1 6 oz. package of noodles
1 vegetarian bouillon cube
3 tbsp. chopped onion
3 tbsp. flour
1/8 tsp. pepper
1 cup each cooked peas and carrots
1 cup cottage cheese
3 tbsp. butter
2 tbsp. chopped green pepper
3/4 cup milk
1/2 tsp. salt
2 tbsp. bread crumbs.

Cook noodles according to directions on package; drain. Dissolve bouillon cube in melted butter. Add onion and green pepper. Cook until tender. Stir in flour and seasonings. Gradually add milk. Cook until mixture thickens. Stir in cottage cheese. Alternate layers of noodles, sauce, peas and carrots in greased 1 quart casserole. Sprinkle with bread crumbs. Bake in moderate oven 375 degrees F until lightly browned.
Serves 4

Cottage Cheese and Onion Surprise

12 oz. cottage cheese, drained dry
1/2 small onion, grated
1/4 cup tomatoes, cut fine
2 tbsp. green pepper, chopped fine
1 tbsp. mayonnaise

Mix all ingredients well, salt and pepper to taste and serve either as a sandwich spread or salad on a bed of lettuce.
Serves 4

Cottage Cheese and Broccoli

2 tbsp. instant onion
1-1/2 cups drained, chopped, cooked broccoli (or spinach)
1/2 cup buttered bread crumbs
2 eggs, slightly beaten
1 cup cottage cheese
1 tsp. salt
2 tbsp. grated Parmesan and Romano cheese
1/4 tsp. pepper

Combine onion, broccoli, cottage cheese, eggs, salt and pepper; blend well. Place mixture in buttered 1 quart casserole. Combine bread crumbs and Parmesan and Romano cheese; sprinkle on top of casserole. Bake in 350 degrees F oven for 35 minutes or until crumbs are golden brown.

Serves 6.

Tomato-Cottage Cheese Spaghetti Sauce

1 package spaghetti sauce mix
1 can tomato paste
1-1/2 cups water
1 tsp. salt
+1/2 lb. vegetarian burger
1 tbsp. instant minced onion
1/2 tsp. salt
2 tbsp. butter
1/2 cup small curd cottage cheese

Blend spaghetti sauce mix, tomato paste, water, butter, salt together in a saucepan. Bring to boiling point and simmer, about 25 minutes, stirring occasionally. Mix burger, onion, salt, in a skillet. Blend burger mixture and cottage cheese into sauce. Serve hot over spaghetti, noodles, or buttered toasted split hamburger buns.

+Worthington Vegetarian Choplet Burger

Cottage Cheese Casserole

2 cups cottage cheese
1 cup each diced cooked carrots, potatoes, celery, onions
1 cup cooked peas
1 cup fine noodles, cooked and drained
1/4 cup melted butter
1 tbsp. seasoning broth
Liquids from cooked vegetables
Biscuit dough

Combine all vegetables, noodles and broth. Make thin gravy from broth and vegetable juices. Fill individual casseroles 3/4 full of vegetable and cottage cheese mixture. Cover with gravy and place small round of biscuit dough over top. Large casserole may be used if desired, and mixture covered with pastry crust. Place in moderate oven, 350 degrees F and bake until biscuits are done.

Serves 6.

Cottage Cheese Souffle

1/2 cup butter
1/2 cup sugar
4 eggs, separated
1 cup cottage cheese
1 cup sour cream
1 tbsp. lemon juice
3/4 cup finely chopped plumped prunes.

Cream together butter and sugar until light and fluffy; add egg yolks and beat until thoroughly blended. Add prunes. Press cottage cheese through sieve; add cheese with sour cream and lemon juice to prune mixture. Beat egg whites stiff; fold into prune mixture. Pour into greased 2 qt. casserole and set in shallow pan of boiling water. Bake in moderate oven 350 degrees F one hour. Serve immediately.

Serves 8.

Spicy Cottage Cheese Pie

1/3 cup undiluted evaporated milk
1 cup water
1/3 cup sugar
4 eggs
1/4 tsp. salt
1 tsp. vanilla
1/4 tsp. nutmeg
1 cup cottage cheese
1 tsp. cinnamon

Combine evaporated milk with water, sugar, eggs, salt, vanilla and spices in a bowl. Beat until smooth. Add well-drained cottage cheese. Mix well. Pour into a single crust unbaked pie shell. Bake in hot oven 425 degrees F about 10 minutes, reduce to moderate heat 350 degrees F and continue to bake about 35 minutes. Cool.

Serves 6.

Cottage Cheese Luncheon Pie

2 eggs
2 cups cream style cottage cheese
2 cups hot mashed potatoes
3/4 cup thick sour cream
2 tbsp. butter
1/4 cup finely chopped onion
2 tbsp. chopped pimiento
1 tsp. salt
1/8 tsp. white pepper
Pastry for 9 inch pie crust unbaked.

Beat eggs until thick and piled softly. Blend thoroughly cottage cheese, potatoes, sour cream, onion, pimiento, salt and pepper. Turn mixture into pie shell, spreading evenly. Dot surface with butter. Bake at 350 degrees F about 1-1/2 hours or until lightly browned. Serve hot or cold.

Serves 8.

Scrambled Eggs with Cottage Cheese

1 tbsp. butter
1/2 tsp. salt
1/4 cup milk
6 eggs, slightly beaten
3/4 cup dry cottage cheese
4 slices toast

Melt butter in frying pan. Stir salt and milk into eggs. Pour into frying pan and cook slowly, stirring occasionally. When eggs are thickened mix in cottage cheese. Serve at once on toast.

Serves 8

Spinach and Cottage Cheese Dumplings

3 cups chopped, cooked spinach
3 tbsp. butter
1 tsp. salt
1-1/4 cups cottage cheese
2 tbsp. flour
3 egg yolks, well beaten
2 quarts boiling water
1 cup grated Parmesan cheese
1/4 cup of melted butter
Dash of pepper and nutmeg

Drain spinach thoroughly. Combine with 3 tbsp. butter, cottage cheese, flour, seasonings, and beaten egg yolks. Chill mixture until cold. Form into balls size of walnuts. Roll in additional flour, then drop into rapidly boiling water. As soon as dumplings rise to top remove with slotted spoon and drain. Serve with 1/4 cup melted butter and cheese.

Makes 1-1/2 dozen balls.

Portuguese Cottage Cheese

2 cups cottage cheese, whipped
6 oz. can mushrooms, chopped
1 tbsp. crushed caraway seeds
1 tbsp. minced capers
1 tbsp. minced chives
1/8 tsp. dry mustard (optional)
2 tsp. paprika

Whip cottage cheese until smooth, adding a little sweet or sour cream if necessary. Blend in chopped mushrooms, then add the other ingredients. Mold this mixture into a mound and sprinkle with paprika. Set in refrigerator to chill for an hour or so. Serve on a bed of salad greens with garnishes of lemon slices.

Serves 4.

Cottage Cheese Meat Cakes

2 cans Soymeat (chicken style) cubed
1 egg
1/4 cup chopped parsley
1 cup creamed cottage cheese
2 tbsp. milk
1 egg
Fine bread crumbs.

Combine soymeat, egg, parsley and cottage cheese. Shape into 2 inch cakes. Beat together milk and egg. Dip cakes into bread crumbs, milk-egg mixture, and again into bread crumbs. Saute cakes in butter until golden brown on both sides. Serve with tartar or tomato sauce.

Makes 12 cakes.

Ukrainian Cheese Cakes

2 cups dry cottage cheese
2 tbsp. sour cream
2 eggs well beaten
1 tbsp. honey
1/2 tsp. salt
2 tbsp. whole wheat flour
2 tbsp. butter
6 tbsp. finely ground hazel nuts

Rub the dry cottage cheese through a sieve. Blend into it the other ingredients, mixing well. Form into flat cakes about 2 inches wide, and saute in melted butter until golden brown on both sides. Serve with cold sour cream or top with raw sugar and a dash of cinnamon and a little grated lemon peel. These wonderful cheese cakes provide a novel breakfast. Ground almonds, sunflower seed kernels or sunflower seed meal may be substituted for the hazelnuts with equally delicious results.

Serves 4.

Cottage Cheese Spoon Bread

3/4 cup milk
1/2 cup corn meal
1 tsp. salt
1 tbsp. sugar
3 egg yolks
3 tbsp. butter
1 cup small curd cottage cheese
3 egg whites

Scald milk. Add corn meal and cook, stirring constantly until thickened. Mix in salt and sugar. Blend in small amount of hot corn meal mixture with egg yolks, then return to saucepan, mixing thoroughly. Stir in butter and cottage cheese. Beat egg whites until stiff but not dry; fold corn meal mixture into them. Pour into buttered 1-1/2 qt. casserole and bake 35 minutes at 375 degrees F. Serve immediately with plenty of melted butter.

Serves 6.

Cottage Cheese Loaf

2 medium onions, chopped
2 tbsp. butter
2 cups cottage cheese
1/2 cup chopped pecans
1/2 cup chopped spinach
1/2 cup cooked rice
1/2 cup bread crumbs
1/2 tbsp. chopped parsley
1/2 tbsp. lemon juice
1/4 tsp. salt
1/4 tsp. pepper

Combine cheese, nuts, spinach, rice, bread crumbs, and lemon juice. Melt butter in a casserole, add onions, and saute until the onions are transparent but not brown. Add to dry mixture and mix well. Season to taste, mold into a loaf, put in a greased baking pan. Bake at 350 degrees for 15-18 minutes. Serve with mushroom sauce.

Serves 8.

Cottage Cheese Walnut Loaf

1 qt. regular cottage cheese
1/3 cup oil
1/2 cup chopped walnuts
5 eggs
3 envelopes George Washington broth
1 onion chopped
4 cups Special K cereal

Mix ingredients as listed; put in flat casserole. Cook at 350 degrees for 1 hour.

Serves 6.

Cottage Cheese Sandwich Treats

3/4 cup cottage cheese
1/2 cup chopped walnuts
1/2 cup chopped dates
White or whole wheat bread

Mix well all ingredients. Let stand for a while to blend flavors. Spread on thin slices of lightly buttered bread.

1 banana in 1/2 inch slices
1/2 cup cottage cheese
Bread

Spread bread slices with cottage cheese, arrange banana slices on top.

1-1/4 oz. Roquefort cheese
8 oz. cottage cheese
1/2 tsp. onion juice
6 tsp. sour cream
Bread

Mix all ingredients together and spread on either white, rye or whole wheat bread for sandwiches.

1 cup cottage cheese
1 cucumber cut in 1/2 inch slices
1 medium onion cut in thin slivers
Bread of choice

Spread bread with cottage cheese, arrange cucumber and onion slivers on slices of bread. Combine slices.

Frozen Cottage Cheese

1-1/2 cups cottage cheese
1-1/2 cups vanilla ice cream, softened
1/4 tsp. lemon extract
1 cup canned crushed pineapple, well drained

Combine cottage cheese and ice cream. Fold in lemon extract and pineapple. Freeze until hard, in freezer compartment. 30 minutes before serving remove to lower shelf of refrigerator until ready to serve.
Serves 8.

Frozen Cheese Dream

2 cups cottage cheese
2 tbsp. lemon juice
1 cup sugar
2 cups sour cream

Press cottage cheese through a fine sieve. Add the lemon juice and sugar and beat until smooth and blended. Stir in sour cream and mix well. Pour into refrigerator tray. When mixture is frozen around edges (about 1/2 inch from edge) turn into a chilled bowl and beat with a cold rotary beater until smooth but not melted. Return to tray and freeze until firm. Cut in 6 pie-shaped wedges, serve with fruit for a dream dessert.

Cottage Cheese Strawberry Frozen Pie

12 oz. creamed cottage cheese
1/4 cup sugar
1/4 tsp. salt
1 cup whipping cream
9 oz. can crushed pineapple, drained
1 baked 9" butter short pie shell
1 tsp. vanilla

Whip together cottage cheese, sugar, salt, vanilla, whipping cream until stiff. Fold in crushed, drained pineapple. Pile mixture in baked pie shell. Freeze for 2 hours. Cut into servings. Top with sweetened strawberries. (Or mixture may be placed in ice cube tray and frozen for 2 hours, then spooned into baked pie shell and topped with sweetened berries.)

Toddlers' Tortoni

16 oz. creamed cottage cheese
1 cup light corn syrup
1 cup milk
1 cup broken macaroons
1/2 cup chopped nuts
1 tsp. vanilla
1/4 tsp. almond extract

Beat cottage cheese until smooth, combine with corn syrup, mixing until well blended. Stir in remaining ingredients. Place paper bake cups in muffin pans; pour cottage cheese mixture in. Freeze until firm.

Serves 6 to 8.

Curried Eggs

3 tbsp. butter
3 tbsp. flour
1 tsp. salt
1 tbsp. grated onion
1 tsp. curry powder
1 cup undiluted evaporated milk
1/2 cup water
6 hard cooked eggs cut in quarters
6 pieces of toast or two cups hot cooked rice.

Melt butter in saucepan over low heat. Add flour, salt, grated onion, and curry powder. Mix well. Slowly add milk-water mixture, stirring constantly until blended and thickened. Add hard cooked eggs. Place toast or rice on each serving plate. Spoon milk-egg mixture over toast. Garnish with paprika.

Onion 'N' Egg Casserole

1 tbsp. butter 1-1/2 cups coarsely chopped onion
1 tsp. salt
1 tsp. pepper
1 tbsp. sugar
4 eggs
1 large can undiluted evaporated milk
1 cup water

Cook onion in butter until slightly brown. Remove from heat. Combine onion, seasonings, sugar, eggs, and evaporated milk and water mixture. Mix well. Pour into buttered individual casseroles. Place in pan of hot water. Bake 350 degrees F about 30 minutes. Serve at once with mushroom sauce.

Egg Stuffed Bread Loaf

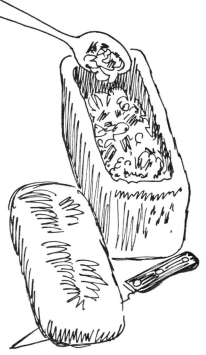

1 loaf unsliced bread
1 egg
1 clove garlic, minced
6 hard cooked eggs chopped
Salt & pepper to taste
1-1/2 cups diced celery or
1-1/2 cups diced green
pepper
1/2 cup mayonnaise
2 tbsp. melted butter.

Cut a slice from top of loaf of
bread and save. Scoop out
enough crumbs from loaf to
make 2 cups. Mix crumbs with
all ingredients, except melted
butter. Fill loaf tightly with
mixture. Add top slice. Brush
with butter, wrap in foil and
bake in hot oven, 425 degrees
F about 30 minutes. Serve hot.
Serves 6.

Egg Vegetable Cutlets

4 eggs, beaten
3 cups cooked mixed
vegetables
2/3 cup uncooked oatmeal
1 tbsp. chopped onion
1 tbsp. salt
2 tbsp. butter

To the beaten eggs, add the
vegetables, oatmeal, onion and
salt. Melt butter in a frying pan
and drop in the vegetable
mixture by spoonfuls. Brown
on both sides. Makes 12.

Poached Eggs on Spinach

1 # 2-1/2 can spinach
1/4 tsp. salt
1/2 stick butter
4 eggs poached
1 recipe savory sauce

Heat spinach, drain and season with salt, pepper and butter. For each serving use about 1/2 cup hot spinach; flatten top and arrange poached egg on each spinach mound. Serve with savory sauce.

Serves 4.

Savory Sauce

1 cup grated cheddar cheese
3 tbsp. butter
3 tbsp. flour
1 cup milk or other liquid
1/4 tsp. salt

Melt butter, add flour, and blend thoroughly. Add liquid gradually, stirring to avoid lumping. Add salt and heat mixture to boiling point, stirring constantly. Add cheese and stir until melted. This makes thick sauce. More liquid may be added if thinner sauce is desired.

Egg Burgers

Split round buns; place on baking sheet. On each top half, place slice of cheddar cheese. Broil until cheese begins to melt and plain halves are toasted. Meanwhile, fry eggs as firm as desired. Place eggs on toasted halves; top with thin onion slices; sprinkle with salt, pepper. Serve at once, open or closed. Serve with chili sauce or mustard.

Creamed Eggs and Mushrooms

6 tbsp. butter
1/4 tsp. ground pepper
2 tsp. minced onion
1/4 cup flour
12 hard cooked eggs quartered
1 qt. milk
2-1/2 to 3 tsp. salt
1 tsp. paprika
1 4 oz. can mushrooms drained
Cream puff shells

Melt butter in chafing dish or double boiler. Add flour and stir until bubbly. Add milk all at once. Cook, stirring constantly, until uniformly thickened. Add the seasonings, onions, mushrooms and eggs. Heat thoroughly. If desired, add more seasonings. Keep creamed eggs' container over hot water while serving. Serve in cream puff shells, garnish with watercress and accompany with boiled rice.

Serves 6.

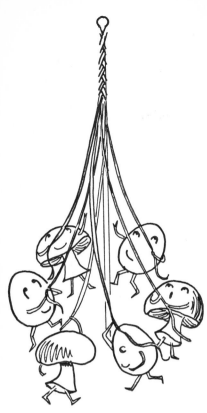

Scalloped Eggs

1 cup cream of mushroom soup
6 hard boiled eggs
1/2 lb. butter, melted
12 soda crackers

Line the bottom of a baking dish with cream of mushroom soup. Then a layer of sliced eggs. Follow with a layer of cracker crumbs which have been rolled in butter, on top. Cook in a moderate oven for about 10 minutes.

Serves 4.

51

Egg Foo Yung

6 eggs
1 medium onion chopped
1 small pepper (green, diced)
1 can bean sprouts, drained
3/4 tsp. salt

Beat eggs in large bowl. Add
remaining ingredients. Ladle
about 1/2 cup of mixture for
each pancake onto lightly
greased griddle. Cook until
golden on bottom, turn and
brown other side. Serve hot
with Foo Yung gravy. Makes 12
patties.

Foo Yung Gravy

1-1/2 cup vegetarian broth
1-1/2 tbsp. cornstarch
1 tsp. soy sauce
1/2 tsp. salt
Dash pepper
1/4 tsp. sugar

Blend broth and cornstarch
in small saucepan. Stir in soy
sauce, salt, pepper, sugar.
Cook over medium heat,
stirring constantly until
mixture thickens. Serve hot.

Pickled Eggs

Strain juice from pickled beets
or sweet pickles; dilute with
water if strong. Use to cover
shelled, hard-cooked eggs.
Refrigerate 1 to 2 days, no
longer.

Spanish Omelet

1 tbsp. butter
1 tomato, diced
1 onion, chopped
1 bell pepper, chopped
5 mushrooms, chopped
6 eggs
3 tbsp. milk
1/2 tsp. salt
1/8 tsp. red pepper
1 tbsp. butter

Saute tomato, onion, pepper and mushrooms in butter. Cook slowly 15 minutes stirring occasionally. Beat eggs with milk, salt and pepper. Melt butter in another pan and pour eggs in. Fry slowly until eggs are set. Pour tomato sauce from first pan over eggs. Fold omelet and turn into a hot platter. Cover with remaining sauce.
Serves 6.

French Omelet

6 eggs
1/2 cup evaporated milk
1 tsp. salt
3 tbsp. butter

Beat eggs until light and foamy. Add milk and salt. Melt butter in frying pan. Pour in egg mixture. Cook slowly. With a spatula, lift up the cooked egg from sides of pan and let uncooked egg run under. Continue cooking and lifting until omelet is of soft creamy consistency. Set in hot oven or under broiler to brown top. Fold and slide onto hot platter.

Serves 6

53

Egg Goldenrod

6 hard cooked eggs
1 tbsp. butter
2/3 tbsp. flour
1/2 tsp. salt
3/4 cup boiling water
3/4 cup evaporated milk
4 slices hot, buttered toast

Remove yolks from 2 of the eggs and press through a sieve. Dice remaining egg yolks and all the egg whites. Melt butter over low heat. Blend in the flour and salt. When smooth and bubbly, stir in water slowly to keep smooth. Cook until mixture begins to thicken, stirring constantly. Add the milk and continue cooking until thickened, stirring all the while. Stir in the diced eggs and reheat. Spoon over toast slices. Sprinkle the sieved egg yolks over top.

Serves 4.

Golden Rod
Plant

Eggs in Potato Nests

1-1/2 cups left over mashed potatoes
eggs
1/2 tsp. salt
1/8 tsp. pepper

Mix potatoes with one of the eggs. Shape mixture into balls, place on greased baking sheet. Press center of balls to make cups. Break an egg in each cup, season with salt and pepper. Bake at 325 degrees F 20 to 25 minutes or until eggs are as firm as desired.

Serves 5.

Hollandaise Sauce

1/2 cup butter
4 egg yolks, well beaten
2 tbsp. lemon juice
1/4 tsp. salt
Dash of cayenne
1/4 cup boiling water

Divide butter into two portions. Place one portion in top of double boiler. Add beaten egg yolks and lemon juice and place over hot water (not boiling) stirring constantly until butter is melted. Add remaining butter and continue stirring until this butter is also melted. Add boiling water to mixture and cook, stirring constantly until thick. Remove from heat and season with salt and cayenne.

Egg Benedict

Cover toasted English muffin halves with thin slices of leftover meat substitute. Top with nicely trimmed poached eggs, and cover with Hollandaise sauce.

Egg Florentine

Put 1/2 inch of hot creamed spinach in the bottom of individual baking dishes. Top with one or two poached eggs and cover with Morney Sauce.

White Sauce

3 tbsp. butter
3 tbsp. flour
1 cup milk or other liquid
1/4 tsp. salt

Melt butter, and flour, and blend thoroughly. Add liquid gradually, stirring to avoid lumping. Add salt and heat mixture to boiling point, stirring constantly. This makes thick sauce. More liquid can be added if thinner sauce is desired.

Morney Sauce

Add 1/4 cup grated Parmesan cheese to each cup of white sauce and allow to melt.

6 Eggs
1 tbsp. butter
2 tbsp. parsley
1/2 tsp. vinegar

Fry the desired number of eggs and remove to a warm platter. Add to the frying pan a tbsp. of butter and (2 tbsp.) parsley for each 2 eggs. Cook slowly 1/2 tsp. vinegar for each 2 eggs. Boil up once and pour over eggs.

Eggs Oriental

1 cup sliced fresh
mushrooms
1/2 cup chopped green
pepper
1/4 cup butter
1 can condensed tomato
soup undiluted
2 tbsp. milk
1/2 cup grated American
cheese
1/2 tsp. Worcestershire
sauce
1/2 tsp. salt
4 hard-cooked eggs sliced

Saute mushrooms and pepper
in butter until tender. Add soup
and remaining ingredients
except eggs. Heat, stirring until
cheese melts; add eggs. Serve
over hot chow mein noodles or
rice.

Eggs a la Creme

Put 2 tbsp. of hot thick cream in
individual dishes, sprinkle with
a little salt and pepper, add 2
eggs and pour a little butter
over the top. Put in moderate
oven 350 degrees F for 3
minutes or until the whites are
milky looking but still soft.

Eggs Provencale

1 eggplant
6 eggs
1/4 tsp. salt
1 cup bread crumbs
2 tbsp. olive oil
2 tomatoes
1/2 tsp. pureed garlic
1/4 tsp. pepper

Slice eggplant, dip in seasoned
eggs and crumbs, and brown
on both sides in olive oil. Top
each slice of eggplant with a
thick slice of tomato that has
been lightly fried in olive oil to
which has been added a few
drops of pureed garlic. On top
of the tomato place a fried egg,
sprinkle with salt and pepper.
Serves 6.

Egg Gourmet

Bake large potatoes, cut in
halves lengthwise, and scoop
out part of the pulp. Place a
poached egg in each half, cover
with Morney sauce and broil
until brown.

Golden Creamed Eggs

1/2 cup grated American cheese
1/2 cup mayonnaise
1/2 cup cooked green peas
1/3 cup milk
1 tsp. grated onion
Dash Tabasco sauce
4 hard-cooked eggs
Toast and crackers

Heat cheese and mayonnaise in top of double boiler until cheese melts. Blend in peas, milk, onion and tabasco. Stir well, heat thoroughly. Save yolks of two eggs, slice whites and other two eggs, add to sauce and heat. Serve on toast or crackers with grated egg yolks over the top.

Eggs Poached in Milk

1-1/2 cups evaporated milk
1-1/2 cups water
6 eggs
6 slices hot buttered toast
1/8 tsp. salt
1/8 tsp. pepper
1 tbsp. butter

Bring milk to simmering point in deep frying pan or shallow saucepan. Break eggs one at a time into a saucer and slip them into the hot milk. Dip milk over eggs with a spoon until whites are set. Lift out carefully with a large slotted spoon and serve on toast. Season with salt and pepper, dot with butter and pour remainder of milk around toast.

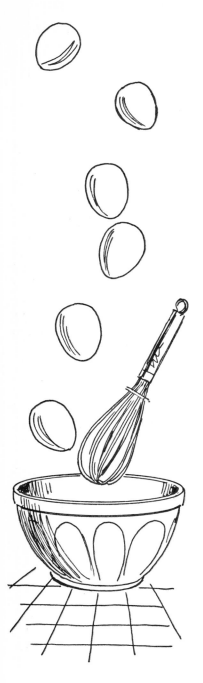

Egg Patties

1 recipe extra thick white sauce+, seasoned with dried parsley
1 dozen coarsely-chopped, hard cooked eggs
2 cups Ritz cracker crumbs
2 sticks melted butter
4 oz. Vegetable oil

Add the cooked eggs to the white sauce. Refrigerate until cold. Spoon into patties, dip in cracker crumbs. Let stand on oiled paper in refrigerator several hours, or overnight. Take out one hour before using. Brown lightly in melted fat, half butter and half vegetable oil.

Souper Eggs

2 tbsp. onion, chopped
2 tbsp. shortening
1 can cream celery soup
1/3 cup milk
Dash Tabasco Sauce
6 eggs, poached
3 English muffins, split
6 slices processed cheese

Cook chopped onion in shortening. Add celery soup, milk, Tabasco; heat. Meanwhile poach eggs, toast muffins. Place slice of process cheese on each split muffin; broil to melt cheese, top with eggs. Pour on sauce, garnish with parsley.

Serves 6.

Spanish Eggs

1 pkg. noodles (5 or 6 oz.)
1/2 cup chopped onion
1/2 cup chopped green pepper
3 tbsp. fat
1/4 cup butter
1/4 cup enriched flour
1 #2 can tomatoes
1/4 lb. (1 cup) grated processed American cheese
1/2 tsp. salt
6 hard-cooked eggs

Cook noodles in boiling water until tender; drain. Cook onion and green pepper in hot fat till tender but not brown. Add tomatoes, simmer 10 minutes, add cheese. Melt butter, blend in flour and salt. Stir in tomato mixture, cook and stir until thick. Place half the cooked noodles in a 2 qt. casserole; slice 3 eggs over the noodles; top with half the tomato mixture. Bake in moderate oven 350 degrees F 25 minutes.

Serves 6 or 8.

Sunday Scramble

1 can any meat substitute
2 tbsp. shortening
6 eggs
1/4 cup milk
1/4 tsp. curry powder

Saute meat substitute in shortening in skillet until brown. With fork beat together eggs, milk, curry, until blended. Pour over meat substitute. Scramble as usual till eggs are creamy and set.

Serves 4.

+Put on remainder noodles, slice other 3 eggs over the noodles; top with remaining tomato mixture.

Curried Eggs Chinois

2 tbsp. butter
2 tbsp. flour
1/2 tsp. curry powder
1/4 tsp. salt
1 small onion
1/2 cup water
1/3 cup light mild molasses
1/4 cup vinegar
1 tbsp. hot prepared mustard
6 hard-cooked eggs

Melt butter in sauce pan; add flour, curry powder and salt. Stir until blended. Add onion and liquids; cook, stirring constantly, until mixture thickens and comes to a boil. Slice eggs lengthwise; mix yolks with mustard; stuff whites. Pour sauce over eggs. Garnish with parsley.

Cottage Egg Scramble

2 tbsp. butter
1/4 tsp. salt
1/2 cup large curd cottage cheese
1/8 tsp. monosodium glutamate
1/8 tsp. pepper
6 tbsp. undiluted evaporated milk
6 eggs

Melt butter in large skillet, In medium bowl with fork beat eggs with salt, monosodium glutamate, pepper, milk, until just blended. Turn into skillet. Cook over medium heat, lifting edges with spoon, until partially set. Stir in cottage cheese; cook until eggs are set but still moist; remove from heat and serve immediately.

Rarebit Scramble

1 tbsp. butter
1/4 lb. grated sharp cheddar cheese
4 eggs
1/4 cup undiluted evaporated milk
1/2 tsp. salt
Dash of pepper
3 tbsp. catsup
2 tsp. Worcestershire Sauce

In double boiler melt butter; add cheese, stirring occasionally until melted. With fork beat eggs with milk, salt, pepper just until blended; stir into cheese. Cook, stirring occasionally, until partially thickened. Add catsup and Worcestershire sauce. Continue cooking until thickened and fairly smooth. Serve on toast.

Serves 4.

Swiss-Style Baked Eggs Au Gratin

1/2 lb. natural Swiss cheese slices
1 cup heavy cream
1/8 tsp. pepper
6 eggs
1/4 tsp. salt
Dash paprika

Start heating oven to 425 degrees F. In well buttered, deep, fluted 9" pie plate, overlap Swiss cheese slices. Pour in cream. Slip in eggs, side by side, add salt, pepper, paprika. Bake 10 to 15 minutes or until done as you like them. Serve on toast.

Serves 6.

Omelet with Spaghetti

3 egg yolks
1/4 tsp. salt
1/8 tsp. pepper
2 tbsp. butter
1 can spaghetti in tomato sauce with cheese
3 egg whites
3/4 cup grated process sharp cheddar cheese

Mix egg yolks, salt and pepper with spaghetti. Beat egg whites until stiff; fold in spaghetti mixture. Heat oven to 375 degrees F. In medium iron skillet, heat butter; pour in spaghetti mixture. Cook over medium heat 10 minutes, or until brown around edge when lifted with fork. Sprinkle top with cheese. Bake 10 to 12 minutes or until cheese is melted and top is brown. To serve cut into wedges.

Serves 4.

New Zealand Style Eggs

3 tbsp. butter
1/4 cup minced onion
1 cup diced, cold cooked potatoes
5 eggs
1/2 cup light cream or milk
1/4 tsp. salt
Dash pepper
2 tbsp. snipped parsley
4 tomatoes, quartered
1/8 tsp. salt
Pinch sugar
1 tbsp. butter

In skillet, saute onion and potatoes in butter until golden brown. With fork, beat eggs with cream, salt, pepper, and parsley just until blended, pour over potatoes. Cook over medium heat, gently scraping mixture from bottom as it cooks, until set but still moist. Meanwhile, lightly sprinkle tomatoes with salt, pepper, sugar; saute in 1 tbsp. butter till tender but still firm. Serve tomatoes arranged attractively around eggs.

Serves 4.

Egg Flapjack

4 eggs
1 tbsp. grated onion
1/3 cup all purpose flour
1/2 tsp. salt
1/8 tsp. pepper
1 tsp. baking powder
1/3 lb. grated process cheddar cheese
1/3 cup salad oil.

Beat eggs; add onion; sift in flour, salt, pepper, baking powder and blend well. Stir in cheese. In skillet, heat part of fat. Drop in large spoonfuls of egg mixture, brown on both sides turning once. Add more fat as needed. Serve at once with canned cranberry sauce or marmalade or bananas sauted in same skillet.

Makes 8 flapjacks.

Oven-Poached Eggs in Tomato Sauce

2 tbsp. chopped green peppers
2 tbsp. butter
2 cups canned or cooked fresh tomatoes
1/8 tsp. salt
1/8 tsp. pepper
8 eggs
1/4 cup grated Parmesan cheese

Heat oven to 400 degrees F. Cook green peppers gently in butter 3 or 4 minutes or until wilted. Add tomatoes, salt and pepper to taste; heat till boiling. Break 2 eggs into each buttered individual baking dish or large baking dish. Spoon boiling tomatoes over and around eggs. Sprinkle with cheese and more salt and pepper. Bake 10 to 15 minutes at 400 degrees F or until eggs are as firm as desired. Serve on or with toast.

Serves 4.

Shortcake Omelet

6 egg whites
3/4 tsp. salt
6 egg yolks
1/4 tsp. pepper
1 tbsp. grated onion
3 tbsp. flour
2 tbsp. snipped parsley
1 can cheese soup made into cheese sauce (see recipe on can)

Start heating oven to 350 degrees F. Grease two 8" layer pans; set in oven. Beat egg whites with salt until stiff but still glassy, beat yolks until well mixed; add pepper, onion, flour, parsley; beat until thick and thoroughly blended; fold into egg whites. Spread mixture in hot pans. Bake 15 minutes or until knife inserted in center comes out clean. To serve: Invert one layer onto serving dish; spread top with small amount creamed mixture of cheese sauce; invert second layer on top. At table, with 2 forks cut or tear omelet into wedges. Pass rest of cheese sauce.

Egg-Salad Casserole

6 or 8 coarsely chopped hard-cooked eggs
1-1/2 cups diced celery
1/4 cup broken pecans
1 tsp. minced onion
2 tbsp. snipped parsley
1/4 tsp. pepper
1/2 tsp. salt
2/3 cup mayonnaise
1/4 lb. sharp cheddar cheese grated
1 cup crushed potato chips.

Heat oven to 375 degrees F. Combine eggs, celery, pecans, onion, parsley, pepper, salt and mayonnaise, tossing lightly. Turn into 4 individual casseroles; sprinkle on cheese, then potato chips. Bake 25 minutes.

Serves 4.

Egg Soubise

1 bunch scallions (2 cups) cut into 1" pieces, or 1 cup sliced onions
3 tbsp. butter
1/4 tsp. salt
1/8 tsp. pepper
6 cut up hard cooked eggs
1 #2 can peas, drained
1 can condensed cream of mushroom soup, undiluted
1/3 cup light cream
Nutmeg, curry or Parmesan cheese
Bite-size shredded wheat

In skillet, saute scallions or onions in butter till tender but not brown. Add salt, pepper, eggs, peas, soup and cream; stir to blend. Heat; sprinkle with nutmeg. Serve topped with bite-size shredded wheat. Pass rest of shredded wheat in basket.

Serves 4.

Oven-Poached Eggs in Tomato Sauce

2 tbsp. chopped green peppers
2 tbsp. butter
2 cups canned or cooked fresh tomatoes
1/8 tsp. salt
1/8 tsp. pepper
8 eggs
1/4 cup grated Parmesan cheese

Heat oven to 400 degrees F. Cook green peppers gently in butter 3 or 4 minutes or until wilted. Add tomatoes, salt and pepper to taste; heat till boiling. Break 2 eggs into each buttered individual baking dish or large baking dish. Spoon boiling tomatoes over and around eggs. Sprinkle with cheese and more salt and pepper. Bake 10 to 15 minutes at 400 degrees F or until eggs are as firm as desired. Serve on or with toast.

Serves 4.

Skillet Eggs Frou-Frou

1/3 cup butter
12 eggs
1-1/2 tsp. seasoning salt
3 cups seasoned sliced mushrooms
1/2 cup sliced stuffed olives

In an electric skillet barely melt butter. Break eggs singly into a saucer and slide into the skillet. Dust with 1-1/2 tsp. seasoning salt. Cover; cook at 320 degrees F until almost firm. Border with 3 cups seasoned, sliced mushrooms butter sauteed with 1/2 cup sliced olives. Garnish, sauteed mushroom caps with capers.

Dinner Casserole de Luxe

5 hard-cooked eggs
1 3 oz. can sliced mushrooms
Milk
3 tbsp. butter
2 tbsp. flour
1/4 tsp. salt
1/4 tsp. onion salt
1/2 cup minced celery
1/2 cup poultry seasoning stuffing
1/2 cup grated cheddar cheese

Heat oven to 375 degrees F. Slice eggs into shallow 1-1/2 qt. casserole or 10x6x2 baking dish. Drain juice from mushrooms into measuring cup; add milk to make 1 cup. In 1 tsp. butter in saucepan, heat mushrooms 2 or 3 minutes, scatter mushrooms over eggs. Add rest of butter to saucepan; melt; stir in flour, salt, then milk mixture. Cook, stirring until thickened. Add celery, pour over eggs. Scatter stuffing, mixed with cheese over top. Bake 20 minutes or until bubbly.

Serves 4.

Polish Souffle

1 cup millet meal
1/4 cup cold water
3 cups boiling salted water
1 tsp. salt
1-1/4 cup shredded sharp cheese
1-1/4 cups thick sour cream or whipped cottage cheese

Prepare a thick hot millet mush by moistening 1 cup of millet meal with 1/4 cup of cold water, then stirring slowly into a scant 3 cups of boiling salted water. Allow to cook in the top of a double boiler for 20-30 minutes or until thick. Stir frequently. When done, cover the bottom of a shallow greased baking dish with half the hot mush. Spread with cheese, and cover with remaining mush. Pour cream or cottage cheese over the top and bake in a 375 degrees F oven for 10 to 15 minutes. Serve hot with a cooked green vegetable, tossed salad and a fruit cup.

Serves 4.

Man-Style Baked Eggs

3 tbsp. butter
2 medium onions, thinly sliced
1/8 tsp. salt
1/8 tsp. pepper
4 eggs
2 tbsp. bread crumbs
4 slices process sharp cheddar cheese.

Heat oven to 350 degrees F. In butter in skillet cook onions about 5 minutes or until just tender. Arrange in 8" pie plate; sprinkle lightly with salt, pepper. Break eggs over onions; sprinkle with salt and pepper, then with crumbs; top with cheese. Bake, uncovered, 10 minutes or until eggs are of desired firmness.

Egg Croquettes

1 can condensed cream of celery or mushroom soup
8 hard-cooked eggs, sieved or very finely chopped
1/4 cup fine dry bread crumbs
2 tbsp. shortening
2 tbsp. minced parsley
2 tbsp. minced onion
1/2 tsp. salt
Dash pepper
1/3 cup milk

Mix 1/4 cup soup with eggs, bread crumbs, parsley, onion, and seasonings; form into 6 croquettes. (If mixture is difficult to handle, chill before shaping.) Roll into additional bread crumbs. Fry slowly in shortening until browned. Meanwhile combine remaining soup with milk. Heat. Serve as sauce over croquettes.

Serves 3.

Bunwiches

3 chopped hard-cooked eggs
3 tbsp. chopped green pepper
1 tbsp. minced onion
Bit minced garlic
1 tbsp. chopped pimento
2 tbsp. butter
2 tbsp. chili sauce
1/8 tsp. salt
1/8 tsp. pepper
2 tbsp. grated cheddar cheese
6 frankfurter rolls

Day before: Mix together eggs, green pepper, onion, garlic, pimento, butter, chili sauce, salt, pepper, and cheese. With fork, scoop out centers of frankfurter rolls; fill with egg mixture. Wrap each roll in foil or waxed paper. Refrigerate. To serve: Heat in 400 degrees F oven 8 minutes.

Serves 6.

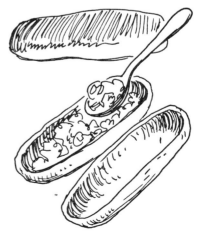

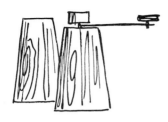

Chili-Nested Eggs

4 hard-cooked eggs
3/4 tsp. onion salt
1/4 tsp. pepper
1 egg yolk
1 egg white
1/2 cup flour
Pkg. dried bread crumbs
1 can chili without beans

About 20 minutes ahead chop eggs very fine; add onion, salt, pepper, egg yolk; mix well, mashing with spoon. Form egg mixture into thick 4-1/2" thick patties. Beat egg white with fork till frothy; dip patties first into flour, next into egg white, then into crumbs. Heat chili over low heat, stirring occasionally. In hot oil in skillet, brown patties on both sides. To serve: Spoon chili into 4 individual casseroles; top each with 1 egg patty. Nice for luncheons with tossed green salad, crisp crackers, tangerines to eat out-of-hand, and hot chocolate.

Serves 4.

Zippy Hot Egg Salad

6 hot hard-cooked eggs
1/4 tsp. salt
1/8 tsp. pepper
3 tbsp. chopped scallions
3 tbsp. snipped parsley
1/4 cup mayonnaise
2 tbsp. catsup or chili sauce
1 tsp. prepared mustard

Into warm bowl, slice hot hard-cooked eggs. Add salt, pepper, scallions and parsley, tossing lightly. Toss in combined mayonnaise, catsup and mustard. Serve on lettuce with hot buttered, toasted rolls or English muffins, or toast.

Serves 3 or 4.

Eggs Creole

3 tbsp. chopped onion
3 tbsp. chopped green
pepper
2/3 cup water
1/3 cup uncooked rice
1 cup grated American
cheese
4 eggs
1/8 tsp. salt
1/8 tsp. pepper

Cook onion and green pepper in butter until slightly browned. Add tomatoes and water; heat to boiling. Add rice, salt and pepper. Cover and cook over low heat until rice is tender. Stir occasionally with fork to keep from sticking. If rice becomes dry, add more water. Drop eggs on rice, taking care not to break yolks. Cover and simmer for 5 to 10 minutes or until eggs are firm as desired.

French Toast

2 eggs
1/2 tsp. salt
1 tbsp. sugar
1/4 cup milk
1/8 stick butter
6 white or whole wheat
bread slices

Break eggs into shallow dish; with fork beat lightly, stir in salt, sugar and milk. Heat a little butter in skillet. Quickly dip bread slices, one at a time into egg mixture; turn until just well coated. In hot butter, brown at once on both sides. Serve immediately with either butter, syrup, molasses jelly, jam, marmalade, honey or applesauce. Sprinkle on confectioners' sugar and lemon juice.

Serves 6.

De Luxe French Toast

Substitute light or heavy cream for milk in the above recipe; add 1 tsp. sherry flavor.

Oven-Style French Toast

Arrange the dipped bread slices on well-greased baking sheet. Bake at 500 degrees F. 5 minutes on each side.

Blue Cheese Burgers

1 can vegetarian burger
1 egg, beaten
1 tsp. salt
1 tsp. onion salt or
hickory-smoked salt
1/4 tsp. pepper
1/4 cup crumbled blue
cheese
1 tbsp. mayonnaise
1 tbsp. softened butter
1-1/2 tsp. Worcestershire
sauce
1/4 tsp. dry mustard

Lightly mix together burger,
egg, and a mixture of salt, onion
salt, pepper; shape into patties.
Blend together the remaining
ingredients; set aside. Grill
burgers in a greased basket
broiler or directly on grill about
3 inches from coals for about 6
minutes on each side. Brush
occasionally with melted butter.
Just before burgers are done on
second side, spread with
cheese mixture. Serve on
toasted buttered buns. Note:
For a quick variation, mix only
blue cheese and burger. Shape
and grill.

Golden Puff

1 "Stack Pack" Premium
crackers
3/4 lb. Velveeta Cheese
Spread, sliced
2 tbsp. chopped onion
2-1/2 cups milk
4 eggs, beaten
1/2 tsp. dry mustard
Dash of pepper

Place half of the crackers in a
12x8 inch baking dish. Cover
with Velveeta slices and onions.
Top with remaining crackers.
Combine milk, eggs and
seasonings, pour over crackers.
Let stand 1 hour and bake 325
degrees F 40 minutes.

Serves 6.

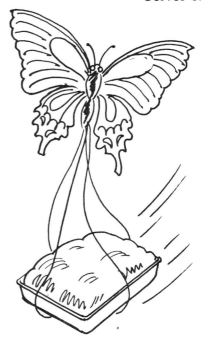

Peanut-Cheese Loaf

2/3 cup cooked whole wheat
cereal or brown rice
1/4 cup chopped green
pepper
3 tbsp. minced onion
1/2 tsp. salt
2 tsp. lemon juice
1 cup chopped peanuts
2/3 cup fine whole wheat
bread crumbs
1 cup grated cheese, any
kind
1 egg
1/3 cup milk

Combine all ingredients. Press
mixture into a greased loaf pan
and bake. Serve hot with
mushroom or tomato sauce.

Cheese Strata

4 eggs, beaten
1-1/2 cups milk
1/4 tsp. salt
1/4 tsp. pepper
Velveeta or Processed
cheese
Bread for six sandwiches

Make sandwiches with thick
slices of cheese. Place in a
shallow, buttered, baking dish
or casserole. Mix together eggs,
milk, salt and pepper. Pour
over sandwiches. Let stand for
45 minutes. Bake in very
moderate oven, 325 degrees F
for 40 minutes or until puffed
and golden brown.

Section III
Substitute Proteins

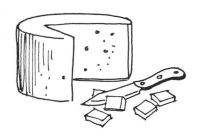

Welsh Rarebit with Indian Flavor

1 tbsp. butter
1 lb. sharp cheddar cheese, shredded
1/2 tsp. Worcestershire sauce
2/3 cup milk
2 tbsp. chutney relish
1/2 tsp. dry mustard
Few grains cayenne pepper
6 slices bread, toasted

Melt butter in top of double boiler over simmering water. Add cheese at one time and stir occasionally until cheese begins to melt. Blend in Worcestershire sauce, mustard, and cayenne pepper. Add milk gradually, stirring constantly until mixture is smooth and cheese melted. Spread tsp. of chutney relish over each slice of toast. Top with cheese mixture. Serve immediately.

Serves 6.

Note: For a heartier dish, top each serving with a poached egg.

Welsh Rarebit

1 lb. sharp cheddar cheese, cut in small pieces
1 tbsp. butter
1 tbsp. mustard, prepared
1 tbsp. fresh lemon juice
1 tsp. Worcestershire sauce
1-1/2 tsp. curry powder

Melt cheese in saucepan, stir constantly. Mix rest of ingredients with melted cheese. Cook for about 12 minutes. Serve on buttered toast points.

Wiener Rarebit

6 tbsp. butter
6 tbsp. flour
3 cups milk
3/4 tsp. salt
1 cup grated American cheese
2 vegetarian wieners, mashed or grated
1/2 cup sliced stuffed olives

Melt butter in saucepan, blend in flour, add milk and cook until thick, stirring constantly. Add salt and cheese, stirring until cheese is melted. Add wieners and olives and heat thoroughly. Serve over hot, buttered toast.
Serves 4.

Tomato Rarebit

2 tbsp. oil
1/2 small onion, chopped
1/3 cup finely cut celery
1/2 small green pepper, chopped
1-1/2 tbsp. flour
1-1/2 cups cooked tomatoes
1/2 tsp. salt
1-1/2 cups grated cheese
2 eggs, well beaten

Melt oil in skillet. Add onion, celery, and green pepper and cook for 8 to 10 minutes or until tender, stirring frequently. Add flour and mix. Add tomatoes and salt. Cook until thickened, stirring often. Remove from heat, add cheese, and stir until melted. Stir some of mixture into beaten eggs. Add to mixture. Pour mixture back into skillet and cook until thickened, stirring occasionally. Serve on toast or crackers.
Serves 4.

Welsh Rarebit

2 tbsp. butter
2 tbsp. flour
1 cup milk
1 lb. sharp cheddar cheese
1 tsp. Worcestershire sauce
Dash salt and cayenne pepper
1 tsp. dry mustard
Toast points

In chafing dish or top of double boiler, make a sauce with the butter, flour and milk. When thickened and smooth, add the cheese which has been cut into several pieces. Stir until cheese is melted. Add the seasonings, using salt and cayenne to taste. Serve hot on crisp toast.

Vegetable Rarebit

10-1/2 oz. pkg. frozen broccoli spears
2 tbsp. butter
1/2 tsp. dry mustard
5 tsp. flour
1/8 tsp. paprika
Dash cayenne
4 oz. can mushrooms, drained
1 cup milk
1 tsp. Worcestershire sauce
1/2 lb. shredded cheddar cheese
6 puff pastry shells

Cook broccoli according to package instructions; drain and cut into bite sized pieces. Melt butter in top of double boiler over hot water; blend in mustard, flour, paprika and cayenne. Slowly add milk and Worcestershire sauce; cook and stir until smooth and thickened; add cheese and heat until cheese is melted. Blend in broccoli and mushrooms; spoon into pastry shells. Toast or cornbread squares could be used in place of pattie shells.
Serves 6.

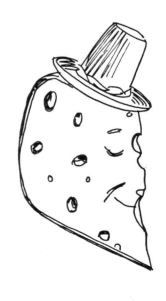

Rapid Cheese Rarebit

Melt jar of processed cheese spread (Cheez Whiz), add 1/4 tsp. dry mustard, dash of Worcestershire sauce. Spoon it, bubbling hot, over Ritz crackers laid edge to edge on bottom and around side of dish.

Luncheon Dish

6 hard-cooked eggs, sliced
1 lb. Velveeta cheese
1 tbsp. milk

Soften cheese in a double boiler with small amount of milk, melt, arrange slices of hard boiled eggs on toast, then pour mixture over. This mixture can also be used when cold as filling for sandwiches.

Kidney Bean Rarebit

2 tbsp. chopped onion
1/2 cup chopped green pepper
2 tbsp. butter
2 cups cooked kidney beans
2 tbsp. catsup
1 tsp. Worcestershire sauce
Dash salt, pepper, cayenne pepper
1/2 lb. Velveeta cheese, sliced
Toast triangles

Saute the chopped onion and green pepper in butter until tender. Add beans, catsup, Worcestershire sauce, seasonings and Velveeta cheese. Cook slowly, stirring until cheese is melted. Serve hot on crisp toast triangles.

Brown Rice Cheese Strata

1 cup brown rice
1/2 pint creamed cottage cheese
2 tbsp. chopped pimento
1 egg beaten
1/4 tsp. salt
1/2 cup diced celery
1/2 cup sliced onion
2 tbsp. butter or margarine
2 cups shredded sharp cheddar cheese
Paprika (dash)
Tomato slices or green pepper rings

Cook brown rice as directed on package. Combine rice, cottage cheese, pimento, egg and salt. Cook celery and onion in butter until onion is tender, not brown. Stir into rice mixture. Spoon half of the rice mixture into 2 qts. casserole; repeat, using remaining rice and cheese. Cover. Bake at 375 degrees F., until hot, 25 to 30 min. Sprinkle with paprika, garnish with tomato and/or green pepper rings.

Devonshire Muffins

Split and toast English muffins and spread halves with Miracle Sandwich Spread. Cover with tomato slice and half slice of Kuminost cheese (Natural Caraway). Broil till cheese melts. Top with onion rings.

Cheese Souffle

4 tbsp. butter
4 tbsp. flour
1-1/2 cups milk
1 tsp. salt
Dash of cayenne pepper
1/2 lb. Old English
Pasteurized Process Cheese,
sliced
6 eggs

Melt butter in top of a double boiler placed over boiling water. Remove from the boiling water, and blend in the flour, salt and cayenne pepper. Gradually add the milk, blending well. Return to the boiling water and cook, stirring constantly, until the sauce is thick and smooth. Add sliced cheese and continue cooking, stirring frequently, until the cheese has melted. Remove from heat and slowly add beaten egg yolks, blending them in well. Slightly cool the mixture, then pour it slowly onto the stiffly beaten whites of eggs, cutting and folding the mixture thoroughly together. Pour into an ungreased 2 qt. casserole. Run the tip of a tsp. around in the mixture one inch from the edge of the casserole, making a slight track or depression. This forms the "top hat". Bake 1-1/4 hours in a slow oven. 300 degrees F. Serve immediately.

Corn and Cheese Souffle

1 tbsp. butter
1 tbsp. chopped green pepper
1/4 cup flour
2 cups milk
1 cup whole kernel corn
1 cup grated cheese
3 eggs
1/2 tsp. salt

Melt the butter and cook the pepper thoroughly in it. Make a sauce out of the flour, milk and cheese; add the corn, egg yolks and seasoning; cut and fold in the whites beaten stiffly; turn into a buttered baking dish and bake in moderate oven 375 degrees F 30 minutes.

Flamingo Souffle

1 cup condensed tomato soup
2 tbsp. butter
1 tbsp. grated cheddar cheese
4 eggs, separated
3/4 tsp. salt
1/8 tsp. pepper
3/4 cup soft bread crumbs

Combine and heat all ingredients except eggs. Remove from heat and add well beaten egg yolks. Fold in stiffly beaten egg whites. Pour mixture into well greased ring mold or loaf pan. Set in shallow pan of hot water and bake slowly at 325 degrees F for about 1 hour.

If ring mold is used, well seasoned and drained canned peas may be poured in center of ring before serving.

Kidney Bean Souffle

3 cups cooked kidney beans
1-1/2 cups grated cheese,
any kind
3 tbsp. catsup
6 egg yolks, well beaten
6 egg whites, stiffly beaten
Few grains cayenne

Press kidney beans through coarse sieve. Add remaining ingredients except egg whites. Fold in beaten egg whites. Pour mixture into greased baking dish. Bake in moderate oven 350 degrees F until set (about an hour).

Mushroom Souffle

1/2 lb. finely chopped
fresh mushrooms
3 tbsp. melted butter
2 tbsp. minced onion
2 tbsp. flour
1/2 tsp. salt
1/4 tsp. pepper
2 tbsp. minced parsley
1/2 cup milk
2 egg yolks, well beaten
1 tbsp. lemon juice
3 egg whites, stiffly beaten

In small skillet to 1 tbsp. melted butter add mushrooms and onion. Cook over slow heat about 5 minutes or until mushrooms are tender but not brown. In small saucepan stir flour, salt, and pepper into remaining butter. Blend well, then slowly stir in milk, and continue stirring over slow heat until mixture boils and is thick. Remove from heat. Add mushrooms, lemon juice, parsley, and beaten egg yolks. Fold in stiffly beaten egg whites. Pour mixture into greased baking dish and bake at 375 degrees F for 30 to 35 minutes or until firm but not dry.
Serves 4.

Pimento and Cheese Roast

2 cups cooked lima beans
1/4 lb. cream cheese
3 canned pimentos, chopped
3 slices bread, crumbed

Put first three ingredients through a meat chopper. Mix thoroughly and add bread crumbs until it is stiff enough to form a roll. Brown in the oven, basting occasionally with butter and water.

Cheese and Soymeat Short Cake

1/2 lb. Velveeta or Kraft American Cheese
1/3 cup vegetarian broth
1-1/2 cups cubed soymeat, chicken style
Baking powder biscuits
1 tbsp. butter
Parsley

Melt the Velveeta cheese in the top of a double boiler. Add broth gradually, stirring constantly until the sauce is smooth. Add the cubed soymeat and mix carefully. Split hot biscuits, spread with butter, then put together with a generous filling of the hot soymeat. Garnish with parsley. Serves 6.

Cheddar Pudding

1 pint milk
1/2 cup farina or cornmeal
1 tbsp. butter
1/2 tsp. salt
1 egg
1-1/2 cups Velveeta cheese, cubed
1 tbsp. butter
1 tbsp. flour
1 cup milk
1/8 tsp. salt
1/8 tsp. pepper

Cook milk, farina or cornmeal, butter and salt in a double boiler as for cereal. When well cooked and thick remove from heat and add the well beaten egg and 1/2 cup of Velveeta cheese. Pour into a shallow greased pan to the depth of 1 inch. When cold, cut into 12 squares and place 3 squares in each of 4 shirred egg dishes. Cover with cream sauce and sprinkle with the remaining Velveeta cheese and place in a very moderate oven, 325 degrees F a minute or two before serving.

Serves 4.

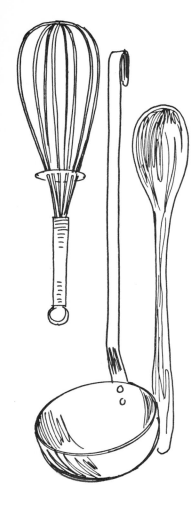

Cream Sauce

1 tbsp. butter
1 tbsp. flour
1 cup milk
1/8 tsp. salt
1/8 tsp. pepper

Mix all ingredients together and stir until smooth.

Swiss Cheese Fondue

1 lb. natural Swiss cheese,
about 4 cups, shredded
5 tsp. cornstarch
1 tsp. cherry flavoring
1 clove garlic, cut in halves
1/4 tbsp. salt
1/8 tsp. pepper
2 cups Catawba juice

Set out double boiler or chafing
dish. Cut 1 lb. French loaf or
Italian bread into bite-size
pieces having at least one crusty
side and set aside. Shred 1 lb.
natural Swiss cheese. Mix
together in a small bowl and set
aside 5 tsp. cornstarch, cherry
flavoring. Rub boiler or chafing
dish with cut surface of garlic.
Put into boiler or chafing dish
the shredded cheese and a
mixture of salt, pepper. Pour
over the cheese the Catawba
juice. Stirring constantly, cook
over medium heat until cheese
is melted. Blend in the
cornstarch mixture. Continue
stirring while cooking 2 to 3
minutes, or until fondue begins
to bubble. Keep fondue gently
bubbling throughout serving
time. Serve at the table. Spear
bread cubes with a fork; dunk
and twirl them in the fondue.
Serves 4.

The Pecan

Cheese Pecan Loaf

2 beaten eggs
1 cup chopped pecans
1 cup whole wheat bread crumbs
1 tsp. salt
2 tbsp. scraped onion
1 tbsp. finely chopped parsley
1 cup grated yellow cheddar cheese
1 cup milk
1 cup celery cut into small pieces

Form into a loaf and bake in well buttered pan in moderate 350 degrees oven for 20 minutes. Serve with mushroom or tomato sauce.

Serves 6.

Tamale Cheese Casserole

1 medium onion, minced
1 clove garlic, minced
1 can choplets-chopped or vegeburger
1/2 lb. American cheese grated
1 can tomato soup
1 tbsp. chili powder
1/2 tsp. salt
1 can red kidney beans

Saute in butter, onion and garlic. Add remaining ingredients. Bake in moderate oven 25 minutes. If desired, decorate with cheese strips last 10 minutes.

Serves 5-6.

Baked Cheese Fondue

3/4 lb. sharp Cheddar cheese
3 cups soft bread cubes
1 tbsp. melted butter
1 tsp. poppy seeds
2 cups milk
3 tbsp. grated onion
1/2 tsp. salt
4 egg yolks, well beaten
1/4 tsp. pepper
1/2 tsp. dry mustard
1/4 tsp. paprika
1 or 2 drops Tabasco sauce
4 egg whites.

Lightly butter 2 qt. casserole. Shred and set aside Cheddar cheese. Prepare bread cubes, toss 1 cup of bread cubes lightly with butter and poppy seeds. Set cubes aside. Scald milk. Pour scalded milk into a large mixing bowl. Add to milk and mix the 2 cups uncoated bread cubes, shredded cheese, onion and a mixture of salt, pepper, mustard, paprika, Tabasco. Mix lightly but thoroughly until cheese is melted. Add egg yolks well beaten, stirring constantly. Beat egg whites until rounded peaks are formed. Spread beaten egg whites over cheese mixture and gently fold together. Turn into casserole. Top with poppy seed and coated bread cubes. Bake in boiling water bath at 325 degrees F 50 to 60 minutes or until a silver knife inserted halfway between center and edge comes out clean. Serve immediately.

Serves 6.

Oven Macaroni

1/4 cup chopped onion
1 tbsp. butter
1 can condensed Cheddar
cheese soup
1/2 cup milk
2 cups cooked macaroni
2 tbsp. buttered bread
crumbs

Cook onion in butter until
tender. Blend in soup.
Gradually stir in milk. In
buttered 1 qt. casserole,
combine sauce and cooked
macaroni. Sprinkle crumbs on
top. Bake in 375 degree F oven
about 30 minutes or until
browned and bubbling.
Serves 4.

Souper Spoonbread

1 can condensed Cheddar
cheese soup
1/2 cup evaporated milk
1/2 cup corn meal
1/4 cup butter
3 eggs, separated
1/2 tsp. salt
1/4 tsp. baking powder

In saucepan over medium heat
stir soup until smooth;
gradually blend in milk. Bring to
boil, stirring. Reduce heat and
gradually add corn meal,
stirring until just thickened.
Remove from heat; stir in
butter. Beat egg yolks until
thick; stir in a few tbsp. soup
mixture. Blend yolks into
remaining soup. Combine salt
and baking powder; sprinkle
over egg whites. Beat until stiff
but glossy. Fold whites into the
soup mixture. Pour into 1-1/2
qt. souffle dish. Bake in a 350
degrees F oven 1 hour.
Serves 6.

Patti-Cheese Bake

1 pkg. noodles
1 can Worthington Patties
2 cans mushroom soup
1 cup milk
2 cups grated cheddar cheese
1 tbsp. butter
1 cup soft bread crumbs
1/2 cup ground pecans
1/2 clove minced garlic
2 tbsp. chopped pimento
1/2 green pepper, chopped

Cook noodles to just underdone. Drain. Add cheese, pimento, green pepper and garlic. Slowly brown patties in their packing oil, chopping with spatula as they brown. Stir combined soup and milk into noodle mixture. Add browned patties (leaving fat in pan) and pecans. Put mixture in large, oiled casserole. To fat in pan add an equal amount of butter and toss soft bread crumbs in it. Spread over noodle mixture. Bake at 350 degrees F until crumbs are browned.

Scalloped Hominy with Cheese

1/2 lb. American cheese, grated
1 cup milk
1-1/2 cups hominy
2 tbsp. butter
2 eggs, well beaten
1/4 tsp. salt
1/4 tsp. pepper

Combine all ingredients; pour into greased baking dish. Set in pan of hot water and bake in moderate oven 350 degrees F for 30 minutes or until firm.
Serves 4.

Cheese-Chili Spaghetti

8 oz. spaghetti
1/2 tsp. salt
1/4 tsp. pepper
3/4 cup grated sharp
Cheddar cheese
8 oz. vegetarian chili (no beans)
1 tbsp. butter
Snipped parsley

About 1 hour before serving, cook spaghetti as label directs; drain. Then start heating oven to 350 degrees F. Toss spaghetti with salt, pepper. In oiled 1-1/2 qt. ring mold or casserole, arrange spaghetti, sprinkle with cheese. Cover mold with foil or cover casserole. Bake 30 minutes. Meanwhile heat chili with butter. Run spatula around spaghetti; unmold onto heated serving dish. Fill or surround with chili. Sprinkle with parsley.
Serves 6.

Cheeseburger Loaf

1/2 cup undiluted evaporated milk
1 egg
1 cup cracker crumbs
1 can vegetarian burger
2 tbsp. chopped onion
1-1/2 tsp. salt
1 tsp. dry mustard
1 tbsp. catsup
1 cup grated American cheese

Blend all ingredients except cheese until thoroughly mixed. Line loaf pan with heavy waxed paper. Place 1/2 cup cheese in bottom of pan. Cover with 1/2 of meat loaf mixture. Repeat with remaining cheese and burger layers. Bake in moderate oven (350 degrees F) about 30 minutes. Allow loaf to stand about 10 minutes before turning out on platter. Remove paper; slice for serving.
Serves 6.

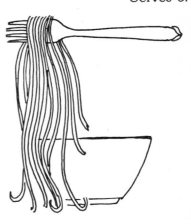

Spanish Sauce

1 tbsp. vegetable oil
2 cups tomato puree
2 tbsp. chopped green pepper
1 tbsp. chopped parsley
1/2 cup onion, chopped
1/2 tsp. salt
Dash of cayenne pepper
1 tbsp. flour
Pinch of red pepper

Cook onion in vegetable oil about 5 minutes. Add tomato puree, green pepper, parsley, and seasonings. Mix flour with a little cold water to make paste and add to mixture. Cook slowly to blend flavor. Chopped mushrooms may be added, if desired.

Cheese and Bean Loaf

1 lb. can kidney beans
1/2 lb. American cheese
1 chopped onion
1 tbsp. flour
1 cup bread crumbs, buttered
2 eggs, well beaten
2 tbsp. melted butter
1/4 tsp. salt
Dash cayenne pepper

Drain beans and put through food chopper together with cheese. Cook onion in hot fat until golden brown. Combine all ingredients except bread crumbs. Mold into loaf. Moisten with melted butter and a little water. Roll in bread crumbs and pack in greased baking dish. Cover with buttered crumbs and bake in moderate oven 350 degrees F for 30 minutes. Serve with Spanish sauce.

Cheese Enchiladas with Tacos Sauce

1 can Enchiladas (tortillas can be used)
3 medium small onions
Green chili peppers, chopped
4 eggs, beaten
Tacos sauce
1 tsp. honey
1 lb. grated sharp cheese
1 tsp. Worcestershire sauce
1/2 cup Parmesan cheese
Few garlic flakes

Mix in large bowl onions, eggs, peppers, Tacos sauce, honey, Worcestershire sauce, garlic and Parmesan cheese. In individual baking dishes place a layer of Enchiladas, a layer of chili peppers, then a layer of cheese. Pour egg mixture over this. Bake in 450 degrees F oven 30 minutes.

Stuffed Green Chili Peppers

Stuff peppers with sharp cheese after cleaning and draining. Dip in egg batter and cracker meal and fry in deep fat. (Banana Sweet Peppers can be used if desired).

Variation: Stuff either green chili peppers or Jalapeno peppers with Philadelphia cream cheese, softened with a small amount of Mayonnaise. Serve with toothpick pinned through each one.

DeLuxe Mock Chicken 'N Cheese

1 can sliced soymeat,
chicken style
1 medium onion, quartered
2 cups cooked wide noodles
2 cups cooked lima beans
3 tbsp. flour
1-1/2 cups light cream
1/2 cup broth
1 tsp. parsley flakes
2 tbsp. diced pimento
1 tsp. salt
1/2 tsp. pepper
6 oz. Cheddar cheese,
shredded

Arrange soymeat in center of 1-1/2 qt. casserole. Surround soymeat with lima beans and arrange noodles around edge. Sprinkle with flour. Blend together cream, reserved broth, parsley, pimento, salt, pepper, sauteed onion and 1/2 of the shredded cheese. Pour over casserole. Sprinkle with remaining cheese. Bake in 350 degrees F oven until cheese is melted and slightly browned, about 20 minutes.

Cheese Waffles

1/3 cup butter
1/2 lb. sharp Cheddar
cheese, shredded
1-3/4 cups sifted flour
1-1/2 tbsp. sugar
1 tbsp. baking powder
3/4 tsp. salt
2 egg yolks
1-1/4 cups milk
2 egg whites

Heat waffle baker while preparing batter.
Melt butter and set aside to cool. Set aside cheese. Sift together into a bowl and set aside: flour, sugar, baking powder, salt. Beat egg yolks until thick and lemon colored. Blend in the cooled shortening, cheese and milk. Add liquid mixture all at one time to dry ingredients; mix only until batter is blended. Beat egg whites until rounded peaks are formed; spread egg whites over batter and gently fold together. Unless temperature is automatically shown on waffle baker, test heat by dropping a few drops of water on grids. It is hot enough for baking when the drops of water sputter. Pour batter into center of waffle grids. It is wise to experiment to find out the exact amount of batter your baker will hold; use that same measurement (spoonfuls or cupfuls) in future waffle baking. Lower cover and allow waffle to bake according to manufacturer's directions, or until steaming stops (4 or 5 min.) Do not raise cover during baking period; then lift carefully and loosen waffle with a fork. Serve immediately with butter and maple syrup. Vegetarian breakfast links may be served with waffle. Cheese waffles may also be served topped with creamed eggs, soymeat (chicken style) or vegetable.
Makes 4 waffles.

For cheese nut waffles follow above recipe. Fold 1/2 cup chopped nuts into batter with the egg whites.

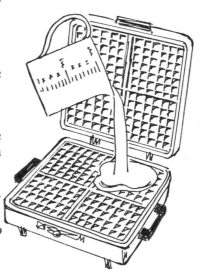

Broiled Cheese-Olive Sandwiches

2 eggs hard cooked
1/2 lb. sharp Cheddar
cheese
1-1/4 cups chopped, pitted
ripe olives
1/2 cup chopped green
pepper
1/4 cup chopped onion
1/3 cup catsup
2 tbsp. mayonnaise
2 tsp. prepared mustard
1/4 tsp. marjoram
1/8 tsp. oregano
1/8 tsp. salt
Few grains pepper
4 buns

Slice into a medium-size bowl hard-cooked eggs. Grate and put into the bowl 1/2 lb. cheese. Prepare and add olives, pepper, onion. Blend together catsup, mayonnaise, mustard and a mixture of marjoram, oregano, salt and pepper. Add to mixture in bowl and blend. Set aside. Set temperature control at broil, 500 degrees F. Split 4 buns and set on broiler rack, cut sides up and place broiler rack in broiler with tops of buns 2 inches from heat source. Toast until buns are golden brown. Remove broiler rack from broiler and spread toasted sides of buns with butter. Spread about 1/8 of cheese mixture on buttered side of each bun. Return broiler rack to broiler with tops of sandwiches 3 inches from heat source. Broil until cheese is bubbly. Serve immediately.

Makes 8 sandwiches.

Cheese Nut Loaf

2 cups coarsely chopped walnut meats
2 cups grated cheese
1 cup bread crumbs
1 cup cooked rice
4 eggs, well beaten
1/2 tsp. each pepper and salt
4 tsp. .chopped onion
4 tbsp. butter
2 tbsp. lemon juice
1-1/2 cups hot milk

Heat butter in skillet and braise onion until slightly brown. Combine cheese, nut meats, salt, pepper, bread crumbs, rice, and milk and add to onion and butter. Mix lightly. Fold beaten eggs and lemon juice into mixture. Place in well greased loaf pan and bake for 45 minutes in slow oven 300 degrees F. Serve with chili sauce or Spanish sauce.

Swiss Cheese Pancakes

6 oz. Swiss cheese
3/4 cup thick sour cream
3 egg yolks, slightly beaten
2 tbsp. plus 1 tsp. flour
3/4 tsp. salt
1-1/2 tsp. thyme
1/2 tsp. dry mustard
2 tbsp. butter.
Set out a heavy skillet. To cheese add 3/4 cup thick sour cream, eggs, slightly beaten. Make a mixture of flour, salt, thyme, mustard, add to cheese. Melt butter in skillet over low heat. Drop batter by tsp. into skillet. Cook over medium heat until lightly browned on bottom. Loosen edges with a spatula, turn and lightly brown other side. Serve at once.

Cheese-Mushroom Scallop

1/2 cup cooked mushrooms, sliced
1/2 lb. sharp Cheddar cheese
6 slices white bread
2 tbsp. butter
1 cup milk
2 eggs
1/2 tsp. salt
1/2 tsp. paprika
1/8 tsp. pepper

Grease 1-1/2 qt. casserole. Set mushrooms aside to drain, reserving liquid. Cut cheese into 1/2 inch slices. Trim crusts from bread and cut into thirds. Arrange some bread fingers on bottom of casserole. Cover with a layer of 1/2 cheese and mushrooms. Repeat layering; top with remaining bread fingers. Dot with butter; add milk to reserved mushroom liquid. Beat eggs until thick and piled softly. Beat in mushroom liquid, salt, paprika and pepper. Pour over layers in casserole. Bake at 325 degrees F 30 to 40 minutes or until puffed and lightly browned.

Serves 6.

Cream Cheese Crepes

1 tbsp. butter
1 cup sifted flour
2 tbsp. sugar
1/4 tsp. salt
6 oz. cream cheese
3 eggs, well beaten
1-1/2 cups milk
1 tsp. grated orange peel

Melt butter in a 6 inch skillet and set aside to cool. Sift together into a bowl and set aside flour, sugar and salt. Beat cream cheese until fluffy, blend in eggs and milk until smooth. Heat skillet; it is hot enough when a few drops of cold water dropped on it dance rapidly in small beads. Pour in about 2 tbsp. batter for each crepe. Immediately tilt skillet back and forth to spread batter thinly and evenly. Cook each crepe over medium heat until lightly browned on bottom and firm to touch on top. Loosen edges with spatula. Turn and brown second side. (It should not be necessary to grease the skillet for each crepe). As each crepe is cooked transfer it to a hot platter. Roll up the crepes and set them in oven to keep warm. When all are cooked, sift over tops confectioners' sugar.
Serves 6 to 8.

Vegetable-Cheese Medley

1 cup hot milk
1 cup soft bread crumbs
2 tbsp. butter
1/2 lb. Velveeta cheese, cubed
3 eggs
1 tbsp. chopped onion
1 tbsp. chopped parsley
1-1/4 cups cooked diced vegetables

Combine the hot milk, crumbs, butter, Velveeta, onion and parsley in top of a double boiler over hot water. Stir until blended. Add the well drained vegetables and beaten egg yolks. Cool slightly. Fold in stiffly beaten egg whites. Pour into a 2 qt. casserole. Bake in very moderate oven, 325 degrees F, 50 minutes, or until set.

Serves 6.

Creole Bean-Cheese Casserole

1-1/2 cups dried lima beans
1/2 tsp. salt
1/3 cup chopped onion
2 tbsp. butter
1-1/4 cups cooked tomatoes, fresh or canned
1 tsp. chili powder
1/2 tsp. salt
1-1/2 cups cubed Velveeta, or shredded processed cheese

Wash the dried beans and soak in warm water 3 hours. Add 1/2 tsp. salt. Simmer until tender; drain. Saute onion in butter until tender. Add tomatoes, chili powder and 1/2 tsp. salt. Cook until slightly thickened. In a casserole, alternate layers of beans, tomato sauce and Velveeta cheese, repeating until all ingredients are used. Bake in a moderate oven, 350 degrees F, 1/2 hour.

Serves 4.

Cauliflower and Choplet Scallop

1 large cauliflower
3 tbsp. butter
3 tbsp. flour
1-1/2 cups milk
1/2 lb. Velveeta or processed cheese
1 cup vegetarian choplets, chopped
1 cup soft bread crumbs
1/8 tsp. each salt and pepper

Separate cauliflower into flowerets, cook until slightly underdone. Add shredded cheese, stir until melted. Place cauliflower in a casserole, sprinkle with choplets. Make a cream sauce of butter, flour and milk and cover the choplets. Make a border of crumbs around edge of the casserole. Bake in a moderate oven, 350 degrees F, 20 to 30 minutes, or until crumbs are lightly browned.

Serves 6.

Potato Casserole

6 or 8 medium potatoes
1 can mushroom soup
1 cup milk
1/2 cup grated American cheese
1 tsp. salt
1/2 cup Parmesan cheese

Parboil potatoes with salt in water until partly tender. Meanwhile mix cream of mushroom soup, milk and cheese in saucepan and heat until well mixed. Arrange potatoes in casserole dish and pour sauce over them. Sprinkle Parmesan cheese over casserole and bake at 400 degrees F for 30 minutes, or until slightly browned.

Scalloped Mock Chicken

1 large sweet pepper
1 medium onion
1 clove garlic
1 stick celery
1 stick butter
1 cup vegetarian broth
1 can mushroom soup
2 cups soymeat (fried chicken style)
1/2 cup bread crumbs
1 package spaghetti

Melt butter, add pepper, onions, garlic and celery; brown. Cook spaghetti; drain. Add browned vegetables, soup, broth, and soymeat. Mix well. Turn into a casserole dish, sprinkle with bread crumbs and brown in oven 350 degrees F. 30 minutes.

Serves 6.

Casserole Italiano

16 oz. vegetarian burger
1/3 cup chopped onion
1 medium clove garlic, minced
1/2 to 1 tsp. oregano
1/2 tsp. salt
1 can tomato soup
1/3 cup water
2 cups cooked wide noodles
1 cup processed cheese, shredded

In skillet, brown onion, garlic and seasonings. Stir in burger, combine this mixture in 1-1/2 qt. casserole with soup, water and noodles. Place cheese around edge of casserole. Bake at 350 degrees F for 30 minutes.

Serves 4.

Broccoli-Cheese Casserole

3 boxes frozen broccoli
1 cup sharp cheese, grated
1 medium onion, chopped fine
4 tbsp. butter
4 tbsp. flour
1 garlic button, minced fine
2-1/2 cups sweet milk
1/2 tsp. salt
1/4 tsp. black pepper
1 egg yolk
Dash red pepper

Cook broccoli until tender and drain. Cook onion and garlic in butter until tender but not brown. Add flour and mix well then gradually add milk and cook slowly until thickens. Remove from fire, add salt and pepper. Beat egg yolk and add part of yolk, then the balance. Also add cheese, stir well. Then pour half of sauce in baking dish. Arrange broccoli on top. Cover with the remaining sauce. Top this with bread crumbs, dot with butter. Bake in oven 400 degrees F for about 20 min., or until it gets hot through and through.

Serves 8.

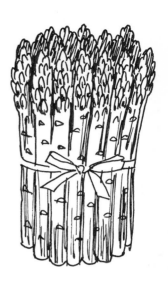

Asparagus Loaf Casserole

1 can cut asparagus, drained
1 cup undiluted evaporated milk
3/4 cup sweet milk
1 cup graham cracker crumbs
1 tsp. minced onion
1 tbsp. melted butter
1 egg, slightly beaten
1/8 tsp. each salt and pepper

Combine milk, crumbs, onion, butter and egg. Fold in asparagus. Place in greased casserole. Bake at 350 degrees F, 30 min.

Sweet Potato Casserole

1 lb. sweet potatoes, cooked
2/3 cup brown sugar
1/4 tsp. salt
1/8 tsp. cinnamon
4 vegetarian vega-links sliced thin
1 small can half slices of pineapple
1/4 cup juice from pineapple
2 tbsp. butter

Boil potatoes in jackets till tender. Slice potatoes lengthwise and arrange on a greased pyrex dish. Sprinkle with brown sugar, salt, cinnamon. Alternate vega-link slices with pineapple slices on top of potatoes. Pour on pineapple juice. Dot with butter. Bake 30 min. in a 325 degrees F oven.

Brown Rice Casserole

3 cups brown rice
1/2 cup safflower oil
1 pkg. onion soup mix
1 cup celery, chopped
6 savita cubes or Bouquet flavoring
8 cups water
6 oz. can mushrooms, sliced

Saute rice in safflower oil until well browned. Add onion soup mix. Dissolve cubes in boiling water and mix with rice. Pour into casserole, pour sliced mushrooms over this and bake until all moisture is absorbed at a temperature of 350 degrees F.

RICE

Family Meal Casserole

1 cabbage
1 lb. vegetarian burger
1 tsp. salt
1/2 cup steel-cut oatmeal
1 egg
3 tsp. catsup
4 tbsp. butter
1/2 onion, sliced
1/2 cup diced celery
2 tbsp. green pepper, chopped
#2 can tomatoes, strained

Put outer cabbage leaves in boiling water for about 3 minutes, drain. Combine burger, salt, oatmeal, egg and catsup and mix well. Put generous serving of mixture into each cabbage leaf, roll securely, tie and fasten with tooth picks. Put into greased pan. Brown in butter, onion, celery, green pepper, add tomatoes. Pour this mixture over cabbage in pan. Then sprinkle grated cheese over cabbage leaves and sauce. Bake in moderate oven of 350 degrees F about 45 minutes. Remove tooth picks and serve.
Serves 6.

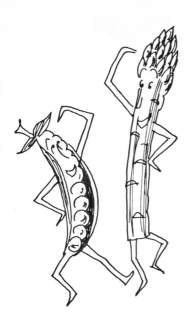

Peas and Asparagus Casserole

1 can green peas
1 can medium asparagus spears
1 can mushroom soup
1/4 cup grated cheese
2 tbsp. butter
Salt and pepper to taste
1/2 cup bread crumbs

Heat soup with 1/4 cup asparagus juice. Add cheese, butter, salt and pepper. Place drained peas in baking dish and cover with asparagus. Pour soup mixture over top and sprinkle with cheese and bread crumbs. Bake 20-30 minutes in moderate oven.

Asparagus Casserole

2 hard boiled eggs
1 pkg. or 1 can green peas
1/4 cup chopped pimento pepper
1 medium can asparagus spears
1/8 tsp. black pepper
1 can mushroom soup or 1 cup white sauce
4 tbsp. butter
1 tsp. salt

Using half the ingredients, put a layer of peas, layer of asparagus, sliced eggs, chopped pimento and pour the mushroom soup or white sauce over this. With the remaining half repeat. Dot butter on top and sprinkle with cracker or bread crumbs and bake 30 minutes in moderate oven.

Corn and Vega-link Casserole

1 can vegetarian vega-links
1/4 cup green pepper, chopped
2 cups whole kernel corn, well drained
2 tbsp. flour
1/2 tsp. salt
2/3 cup undiluted evaporated milk
1/2 cup American cheese, grated
6 tomato slices

Saute in small amount of butter, pepper, until done. Add to corn in buttered 1-1/2 qt. casserole. Blend 2 tbsp. butter with flour and salt over medium heat. Slowly add milk and simmer 2-3 minutes or until thickened. Stir occasionally. Pour over casserole. Top with grated cheese and tomato slices. Bake in moderate oven 350 degrees F, 30 to 35 minutes.

Steaklet-Rice Casserole

1 can steaklets, diced
1 cup rice, uncooked
2 cups cold water
1/2 tsp. salt
3 tbsp. oil
1 can celery soup
1 cup cheese, grated
1/2 cup corn flakes
1/2 cup breading meal

Combine rice, water and salt. Cover and simmer 15 minutes. Meanwhile, dip steaklets in egg and milk mixture, then in breading meal. Saute in oil until lightly brown. Remove from skillet and place half of the steaklets in the bottom of casserole. Mix boiled rice with soup and 3/4 of the cheese. Pour into casserole and top with remaining steaklets and grated cheese. Sprinkle corn flakes on top and bake until done.

Serves 8-10.

Proast Casserole

1 can Proast, chopped
1 cup onions, chopped
2 cups celery, chopped
1 tsp. salt
8 oz. pkg. noodles
1/3 cup cheese, grated

Simmer onions and celery in small amount of salted water until tender. Cook noodles according to directions on package. Drain and rinse. Mix all together. Put in oiled casserole and top with grated cheese. Bake 1 hour at 350 degrees F.

Mock Chicken Casserole

1 cup celery, chopped
1 large onion, chopped
1 green pepper, chopped
3 medium size carrots, thinly sliced
2 or 3 cups soymeat, fried chicken style, diced
1 cup raw rice
2 tbsp. butter
3 cups vegetarian broth
Salt and pepper to taste

Mix all ingredients in casserole dish. Bake covered for 1 hour and 15 minutes at 350 degrees F.

Cheese and Spinach Casserole

2 cups fine noodles, cooked
2 cups cooked or canned spinach, drained and chopped
1 cup grated American cheese
2 tbsp. butter or margarine
2 tbsp. flour
1/2 cup dry skim milk
1/2 tsp. salt
1/4 tsp. pepper
2 cups water

Place half the spinach in a greased baking dish and cover with half the noodles. Sprinkle with half the cheese. Add layers of the rest of spinach, noodles and cheese. Melt butter. Remove from heat. Mix flour, dry skim milk, salt and pepper. Add to butter blending well. Add water, a small amount at a time, mixing well each time. Cook over low heat, and keep stirring until thickened. Pour sauce over noodles and spinach. Bake in moderate oven 375 degrees F, 45 minutes or until top is brown.
Serves 5.

Chili Stew

2 Irish potatoes, cooked and cubed
2 carrots, cooked and cubed
Chili powder to taste

Cook cubed potatoes and carrots, add chili powder. Heat.
Serves 2.

Suggestion

Oatmeal or millet may be used in croquettes, vegetarian meat loaves, burgers, vegetarian meat patties and casserole dishes in place of bread or cracker crumbs. Added to soups, broth and stews oatmeal and millet enrich the flavor and increase food value.

String Bean Casserole

1 can string beans
1 can French fried onions
1 can mushroom soup

In casserole dish put 1/2 beans, 1/3 onions, 1/2 soup, the remaining half of beans, 1/3 onions and 1/2 soup, top with the remaining onions. Bake in 350 degrees F oven for about 30 minutes.
Serves 4.

Polenta Casserole

1 can vegetarian chili
Corn meal mush
1/2 cup cheese, grated

Place chili in casserole, top with slices of corn meal mush, sprinkle with cheese. Bake until cheese melts and browns.
Serves 4.

Corn Chip Pie Casserole

7 oz. pkg. corn chips
1/2 lb. hoop cheese, grated
1 small onion, sliced
1 can vegetarian chili
1/2 cup water

Place small amount of corn chips on bottom of casserole dish, half can of chili, sliced onion, half of grated cheese. Make second layer of corn chips, rest of chili, grated cheese. In center of casserole place a small amount of corn chips, sprinkle lightly with cheese, add water to fill casserole. Place in 350 degrees F oven for 45 minutes. Serve hot.

Serves 4.

Burger and Potatoes Casserole

1 can vegetarian burger
1/2 cup finely chopped onion
1 tbsp. melted butter
1-1/2 tsp. salt
2 tsp. dry mustard
1/4 tsp. pepper
1 tbsp. flour
2 tsp. horseradish
1/4 cup catsup
1 cup chopped celery
1 cup undiluted evaporated milk
1 pkg. instant mashed potatoes

Saute onion in shortening. Remove from heat and mix with burger. Add seasoning, flour, horseradish, catsup, celery and evaporated milk. Place burger mixture in bottom of two quart casserole. Prepare potatoes according to package directions. Spoon over burger. Bake in moderate oven, 350 degrees F about 30 minutes.

Serves 6.

Cheese-Mushroom Casserole

4 oz. can sliced mushrooms, drained. Save liquid
1/2 lb. sharp Cheddar cheese cut in slices
6 slices white bread, trim crusts and cut in thirds
2 tbsp. butter
1 cup milk or cream
2 eggs
1/2 tsp. salt
1/8 tsp. pepper
Tsp. paprika

Grease 1-1/2 qt. casserole. Arrange bread fingers on bottom of casserole. Cover with layer of 1/2 each cheese and mushrooms. Repeat layering; top with remaining bread fingers. Dot with butter. Add together reserved mushroom liquid, milk, salt, paprika and pepper. Beat eggs until thick and piled softly. Beat in mushroom liquid. Pour over layers in casserole. Bake at 325 degrees F, 30 to 40 minutes or until puffed and lightly browned.

Serves 6.

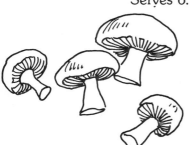

Old Fashioned Corn Scallop

2 cups cream-style corn
2 tbsp. finely chopped onion
2 tbsp. finely chopped green pepper
1 cup coarsely broken crackers
2/3 cup undiluted evaporated milk
1/4 tsp. salt
2 tbsp. butter
1/4 tsp. pepper

Mix corn, onion and green pepper in bowl. Place half of mixture in bottom of a buttered 1 qt. casserole. Sprinkle half the cracker crumbs over corn. Add remaining corn and top with crackers. Mix evaporated milk, salt and pepper. Pour over corn. Top with butter and bake in moderate oven, 350 degrees F, 30-35 minutes.

Serves 4-6.

109

Millet Casserole

1 onion, chopped
3 stalks celery
1 can vegetarian burger
1 tsp. salt
1 cup hulled millet
1 can mushroom soup
3 cans water
1 can mushrooms
1/2 cup sunflower seeds

Saute onion and celery. Add burger, millet, salt. Mix in bowl mushroom soup, water and sunflower seed. Add millet mixture. Put in 1-1/2 qt. casserole. Bake 1 hour at 300 degrees.

Millet Casserole #2

1 cup whole grain millet or millet grits
4 cups hot water
1-1/2 tsp. salt
2 eggs
1-1/3 cups diluted cream or 1 part cream to 2 parts water
1 cup grated cheese

Pour millet in heavy pan, add hot water and salt. Bring to boil, stirring constantly. When millet begins to thicken turn fire very low and cover with close lid. Cook until done, about 30 minutes; (for whole grain millet; about 15 minutes for grits). Beat eggs well, add diluted cream, and cheese. Stir small amounts of cooked millet into egg mixture until all has been added. Mix well. Pour into oiled casserole, sprinkle generously with paprika, dot with butter and bake until set in 300 degrees F. oven.

Millet Italian Polenta

1 cup millet
3 cups water
1-1/2 tsp. salt
2 eggs
1-1/4 cups cheese
1 cup tomatoes
1/2 can tomato sauce
1/2 can celery
1/2 cup onions
1/2 cup green peppers

Cook millet in water until done. Beat eggs well with tomatoes. Stir finely chopped vegetables into millet, add eggs and tomatoes then 1 cup cheese. Mix with fork. Pour into casserole, top with 1/4 cup cheese and bake in 350 degrees F oven until cheese is melted.

Serves 6.

Eggplant Casserole

2 eggplants (1/2" slices)
1/2 cup green pepper
3/4 cup onion
2 cups canned tomatoes
3/4 cup celery
8 oz. Mozzarella cheese
1 cup grated Parmesan cheese
2 eggs (slightly beaten)
Salt and pepper to taste

Dip in seasoned flour slices of eggplant, brown in oil. Saute onions, celery, bell pepper, and add tomato sauce (10 minutes). Layer into greased baking dish: egg plant slices, sauce, thin slices of mozzarella cheese mixed with eggs.
Bake 350 degrees F for approximately 1 hour.

Sicilian Macaroni and Eggplant Casserole

1 eggplant
2 tbsp. olive oil
1/2 lb. macaroni twists
3/4 tsp. salt
1 tsp. dried oregano
1/2 tsp. dried basil
1/2 cup pine nuts
1/2 cup grated Parmesan cheese
1 can tomatoes
2 tbsp. butter

Cut unpeeled eggplant into 1/4 slices. Heat 1 or 2 tbsp. olive oil in skillet. Cook eggplant in it until well browned on both sides, adding more oil as necessary. Cook and drain macaroni. Butter a 2 qt. casserole. Arrange one-half of the macaroni on bottom. Top with 1/2 eggplant. Sprinkle with one half of the salt, oregano, basil, pine nuts and Parmesan cheese. Repeat layers, using the same quantity of ingredients. Top final layer with tomatoes. Dot with butter and bake in moderate oven, 350 degrees F, 30 minutes.

Serves 4.

Eggplant Special Casserole

1 eggplant
1 egg, beaten
1 tbsp. milk
1 cup bread crumbs
1/3 cup shortening
1 onion, chopped
1/4 cup diced green pepper
1 can cream mushroom soup
1/2 cup milk
1/2 tsp. salt
1 cup grated cheese

Peel eggplant and cut in 1/4 inch slices. Combine egg and milk. Dip slices of eggplant in mixture, then in bread crumbs, reserving 1/4 cup crumbs for topping. Brown eggplant slowly in hot oil in skillet. Remove to baking dish. Brown onion and green pepper in skillet, add soup, milk, salt and 2/3 cup cheese. Simmer until cheese is melted. Pour over eggplant. Sprinkle remaining cheese and crumbs over top. Bake in moderate oven 350 degrees F for 30 minutes or until eggplant is tender.

Serves 4 to 6.

Soya Granules Casserole

2 cups Soya Granules, cooked
1 cup carrots, cooked
1 cup celery, cooked
1 cup stewed tomatoes
2 tsp. vegetarian broth
2 tbsp. minced parsley
Toast crumbs for topping

Mix ingredients and pour into greased casserole. Top with toast crumbs and bake until brown. Dot with butter, serve.

113

Southern Onion Casserole

3 cups small whole onions
1 qt. boiling water
1 tsp. salt
2 tbsp. butter
2 tbsp. flour
1/4 tsp. oregano
1/2 tsp. curry powder
1/2 tsp. salt
2/3 cup undiluted evaporated milk
1/2 cup peanuts
1/2 cup grated cheese or soft buttered bread crumbs

Place onions in boiling salted water. Cook 5 to 10 minutes until partially cooked. Drain thoroughly. Melt butter in top of double boiler over low heat. Add flour and seasonings. Stir until smooth. Slowly add milk. Place over boiling water. Cook until thickened and smooth (about 10 minutes) stirring constantly. Add onions and peanuts. Mix well. Place milk and onion mixture in 1-1/2 qt. casserole, greased. Top with grated cheese or buttered bread crumbs. Bake in moderate oven 350 degrees F about 15 minutes. Serve at once.

Serves 4.

Fritos Chili Casserole

3 cups Fritos corn chips
1 large onion, chopped
1 can chili, vegetarian
1 cup grated American cheese

Place 2 cups Fritos corn chips in a 2 qt. casserole. Arrange chopped onion and half of grated cheese on top. Pour chili over onion and cheese. Top with remaining Fritos corn chips and grated cheese. Bake at 350 degrees F for 15-20 minutes

Serves 6.

Bean Sprout Casserole

2 cups canned bean sprouts
1 can whole-kernel corn
4 tbsp. minced green pepper
Seasoning to taste
Melba toast crumbs

Mix cooked sprouts, corn and pepper. Season to taste, almost cover with white sauce. Top with Melba toast crumbs and bake in moderate oven 25 minutes.

Serves 4.

Stakelet Casserole

1 can vegetarian stakelets, save juice
1 egg
1 cup potato meal, crumbs or flour
2 tbsp. cooking oil
2 potatoes, baked
1 onion, sliced

Dip stakelets in egg batter and roll in potato meal, crumbs or flour. Brown stakelets in fat in skillet. Place stakelets in a casserole dish with baked potatoes. Top with slices of onion. Then pour the juice from the stakelet can over the entire contents of the casserole. Bake for 30 minutes at 350 degrees. Serve with green peas and corn on the cob.

Serves 6

Scalloped Noodle Dish

4 hard cooked eggs, cut in eights
1 cup finely cut American cheese
1 cup cooked, fine noodles
1/2 cup stuffed olives, halved
Buttered bread crumbs, for topping
1 can cream of mushroom soup
1/2 cup milk
Salt to taste.

Thin mushroom soup with milk, set aside. Combine all ingredients but buttered bread crumbs in a well greased casserole. Then pour mushroom mixture over this and bake in moderate hot oven, 375 degrees F for 30 minutes.
Serves 6.

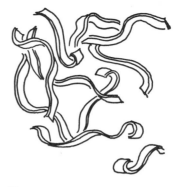

Special Casserole

1 can vegetarian Chicketts
6 oz. can mushrooms
1/2 cup butter
1 cup celery, chopped
1 cup onion, chopped
1/2 cup green peas, cooked
1 cup grated cheese

Drain Chicketts, reserving liquid. Braise celery and onion in butter in covered skillet. Cut mushrooms and Chicketts in small pieces and add, together with salt, to braised mixture. Continue cooking for 45 minutes over slow heat. Remove cover and cook until golden brown. Combine with drained noodles, peas and Chickett liquid. Place in greased casserole, cover with cheese and bake in moderate oven 350 degrees F for 15 or 20 minutes, or until cheese is melted. Overcooking will cause cheese to toughen.
Serves 6.

116

Fritos Zippy Cheese Bake Casserole

1-1/2 cups milk
2 eggs, slightly beaten
1/2 tsp. dry mustard
1-1/2 tsp. salt
1/4 tsp. cayenne pepper
1 cup chopped onion
2 cups grated American cheese
1 cup crushed Fritos corn chips (measured after crushing)

Add heated milk to slightly beaten eggs and seasonings. Mix onion, cheese and Fritos corn chips together and pour into greased 2 qt. casserole. Pour milk and eggs over this. Bake at 325 degrees F for 20 minutes.

Makes 6-8 servings.

White Sauce

3 tbsp. butter
3 tbsp. flour
1 cup milk or other liquid
1/4 tsp. salt

Melt butter, add flour and blend thoroughly. Add liquid gradually, stirring to avoid lumping. Add salt and heat mixture to boiling point, stirring constantly. This makes thick sauce; more liquid may be added if thinner sauce is desired.

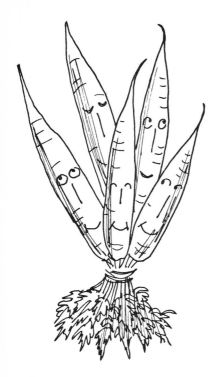

Carrot Loaf Casserole

2 cups cooked, mashed carrots
2 eggs, well beaten
1/4 cup cream or evaporated milk
1 tbsp. sugar
1/2 tsp. salt
1/4 tsp. pepper

Combine all ingredients and mix thoroughly. Place in greased casserole or ring mold. Set in pan of hot water and bake for 45 minutes in moderate oven, 350 degrees F. Turn out on hot platter. Creamed mushrooms may be served over each portion; or if ring mold is used, center may be filled with any desired vegetable just before serving.
Serves 4.

Hominy Casserole

1 gallon well-drained hominy
2 qt. medium white sauce, well seasoned
2 lbs. cheddar cheese, grated
1-1/2 cups finely chopped green pepper
1 to 1-1/2 tbsp. dry mustard

Save 1/4 of the cheese for topping. Combine all other ingredients in an oiled pan. Bake 375 degrees F for 30 minutes.
Serves 30.

Tomato-Macaroni Casserole

2/3 cup undiluted
evaporated milk
1/2 tsp. salt
1 tsp. dry mustard
1 tbsp. Worcestershire sauce
2 cups grated processed
American Cheese
1/4 cup diced green pepper
2 tbsp. grated onion
1-1/2 cups diced fresh
tomatoes or well-drained
canned tomatoes
4 cups cooked macaroni

Simmer milk, salt, mustard and
Worcestershire sauce in
saucepan over low heat to just
below boiling point (2 or 3
minutes). Add cheese and stir
until thickened and smooth (1
to 2 minutes longer). Combine
remaining ingredients in a large
mixing bowl. Add cheese
sauce. Mix thoroughly. Place in
buttered casserole. Bake in
moderate oven 350 degrees F
about 15 or 20 minutes.

Serves 4.

Bon Appétit!

Recipe Notes

Recipe Notes

Recipe Notes

Recipe Notes

Recipe Notes

Recipe Notes

Recipe Notes

Recipe Notes

Recipe Notes